Norfolk & Suffolk
in the
Great War

Norfolk & Suffolk in the Great War

Edited by
Gerald Gliddon

GLIDDON BOOKS
NORWICH NORFOLK

Published 1988 by
Gliddon Books

ISBN 0 947893 07 5

Typeset by Waveney Typesetters (Norwich)
and printed in Great Britain by Biddles Ltd of Guildford, Surrey

Contents

Preface

Norfolk and Suffolk in the Great War is a collection of essays each of which deal with a different aspect of the history of the two counties during the period 1914–18. Inevitably there is some overlap with the history of other East Anglian counties but it is Norfolk and Suffolk which have been primarily studied.

Each of the eight chapters have been specially commissioned for this volume and have therefore not been published before. The main subjects covered include the threat of a coastal invasion, the first bombing raids on the British mainland, the recruitment of the local regiments, the changing face of agriculture, the early days of flying and of airships, case studies of Norwich, Lavenham and Attleborough and a tribute to five men from each of the two counties who gained the highest military honour the Victoria Cross.

Subjects that might be more written about in a future volume include the working of local tribunals in dealing with men who thought themselves unable to fight for one reason or another, the changing role of women which was accelerated during the war years and the birth and testing trials of the tank at Thetford which made its first appearance during the Battle of the Somme in September 1916.

I would like to thank several people who have substantially contributed to the publication of this book and they include Ronald Blythe for agreeing so readily to write a foreword which turned out to be both personal and literary, the five contributors and an extra word of thanks to Peter Kent who not only wrote two of the chapters but also designed the book's jacket. I would also like to thank Steve Snelling for his help with tracking down suitable photographs of the V.C. holders, Wynne Gliddon and Richard Denyer for helping out with the rest of the illustrations. For permission to quote extensively from the War Memorial Book at St Peter and St Paul's Church in Lavenham I would like to thank the Rector the Reverend D. W. W. Pearce and his Churchwardens.

Finally I would like to stress that any mistakes in the text are my responsibility.

Gerald Gliddon, Norwich

Foreword

by
Ronald Blythe

Personal and literary understandings and concepts of what happened to East Anglia during 1914–18 far outweigh my knowledge of the actual facts and figures. I haven't read the official history, regimental or otherwise. But being born only a few years after the Armistice, I was born like every other East Anglian child of my generation into the war's residue, both emotional and physical. My father fought with the 5th Suffolks at Gallipoli, a teenager from a village, and although he was spare with his memories, the litter of medals, puttees (sometimes worn in the fields on wintry days), greatcoat, official Bible and brown snapshots of Egypt hung around the house, profoundly romantic. And there was scarcely a relative's or a neighbour's home where cabinet-size photographs of soldiers and sailors, most of them dead, did not dominate the room. The faces contained an innocence not seen today. It was the innocence of the young countryman of the late nineteenth century – a different race. The grainy, enlarged prints in their polished frames were for me icons through which I could gaze into the previous era. My father never wore his medals, nor did he attend the flamboyantly grave services at the local war memorial. All around us were ex-officers trying to make a go of small farms, smallholdings, especially poultry. It was the return of the agricultural depression after the wartime subsidies had been withdrawn. The ex-officers and their large families lived in ex-military huts made of brick and asbestos which stood in three or four acres of land.

There must have been much talk about the war but little of it filtered through to me and it wasn't until Munich that the Great War lost its almost mystic absence of definition and shot into sharp focus. Much later I began to encounter, sometimes briefly, but once or twice lastingly, the men who made the war actual to me, its writers and artists. I met R. H. Mottram, then in his late sixties, but who in 1924 began to publish *The Spanish Farm Trilogy*, the first volume of which was filmed as *Roses of Picardy*. Mottram was a Norwich bank clerk who served as an interpreter with the Norfolk Regiment and who had been encouraged to write by Galsworthy. He was a lean, formal, courteous man whose manner gave little indication of his poetry, so to speak. Like so many East Anglians, he combined a high imagination with an earthy commonsense. About this time, the early 1950s, I also met Edmund Blunden, who although born in Kent had Suffolk roots, and had made his home at Long Melford. His classic *Undertones of War* (1928) is prefaced with a kind of apologetic fear about daring to go over the ground again a decade after the event. His inspiration came from Thomas Hardy's *The Dynasts*. When I listened to Blunden reading from *Undertones of War*, both the prose part and the handful of Western Front poems with which it concludes, there could be no doubt that he had got his truths right. 'Why should I not write it?' he asks himself. 'I know that the experience to be sketched in it is very local, limited, incoherent . . . I know that memory has her little ways, and by now she has concealed precisely that look, that word, that coincidence of nature without and nature within which I long to remember . . .' The experience was that which was common to most of those who left Suffolk and Norfolk for France and Belgium, although no common hand could record it. However, when I began to listen to First World War voices for my books, I was moved and astounded by the articulacy. Blunden had given himself a pause of ten years in order to get it all into perspective: my talkers had it all, brilliant and pat, after a long lifetime. They had not only known the trenches but had been brought up in the last years of the ancient Suffolk storytelling tradition. They possessed narration as well as memories – and there are many who do not.

I came closest to the war via my friendship with John Nash. He served as a sergeant in the Artists Rifles and in the spring of 1918 he was commissioned as an official war artist. After years of fighting in the trenches, he settled down to painting the war in a seed shed in Buckinghamshire, along with his brother Paul. John Nash's masterpiece, *Over the Top*, in which the cumbersome young figures clambering across the lip of the trench into a snowy no-man's-land has for me the curious and sad underlying suggestion of farmworkers going home after a bitter day of ditching. He talked a lot about both wars, and with care and accuracy. He told me that when he was painting the Great War pictures the War Office offered to return him to the Front 'to refresh his memory'. He was astounded, for like most artists and writers he knew that to have and to hoard experience was the only guarantee of getting things right. But it was indicative of his need to be honest about the Front that he asked for a lorry-load of duckboards, barbed wire, corrugated iron, etc. to be sent to the seed-shed studio so that his pictures would be accurate down to the last barb. As with so many soldiers, the war hung about him for life, hateful and yet beloved. Just before its outbreak he had walked in Norfolk with the artist Claughton Pellew and it was then that he decided to be a painter. After his death I took his badges and the bits of uniform which remain after years of gardening, plus his palette, to the Imperial

War Museum, a rite which would have amused him.

Today, whenever I think of 1914–18 in local terms, the main structure of its history fragments into vivid and isolated scraps. The murder of Edith Cavell and the words and attitude which, had she suffered a similar fate in the Middle Ages, would have made her a saint. The 1917 call-up of the previously reserved class of farm-labourers whose names figure largely on the rural memorials, and whose fate is matchlessly described in Edward Thomas's poem *As the Team's Head-Brass*.

> '. . . Have many gone
> From here?' 'Yes.' 'Many lost?' 'Yes, a good few.
> Only two teams work on the farm this year.
> One of my mates is dead. The second day
> In France they killed him . . . Now if
> He had stayed here we should have moved the tree.'

The sightings of Zeppelins and the haphazard ruin caused by their bombs along our coast are somehow not diminished by the infinitely more terrible 1940–45 raids, but hold their own as high drama. Another bit of the war's local minutiae which sticks in my mind is the role played by men of the First Norfolks during the famous 'Christmas Truce' of 1914 when, much to the generals' horror, the Germans and the British left their trenches, shook hands, exchanged gifts and sang carols. Between 200 and 400 Norfolk men and Germans met in no-man's-land and talked, not of the war but of Christmas. The writer Henry Williamson took part in this truce and it was one of the things which created in him a complex admiration for Germany which was to lead him into strange paths when Hitler came to power. His long novel sequence, based on his diaries, *A Chronicle of Ancient Sunlight*, contains brilliant accounts of the Front and of Mosley-ite East Anglians between the wars. I recall too Suffolk efforts to retain the war's precious camaraderie, the springing up of all sorts of clubs which in those stagnant and bitter days doled-out food, small sums of money and second-hand clothes to the neglected ex-servicemen. In my book about old age, *The View in Winter*, I tried to penetrate the mysteries of Toc-H and what this Christian cult, founded for those fighting on the Ypres Salient, and to hear what it still meant for some very old soldiers. Toc-H, the British Legion, Old Comrades' Associations, regimental dinners and a host of other 1914–18-remembering societies had a considerable social effect on East Anglian life.

But so they did elsewhere. And this for me is the now impossibility of seeing the world wars in parochial terms. I can only recognise the Suffolk element by looking at what happened in 1914 through a child's eye. My adult gaze slots these impressions into the full historic context, or into what I can only call poetry. A poetry which so far has not got on to the page. My moral mentor on the vast tragedy remains Wilfred Owen and there is very little of what this Welsh-border voice uttered on the subjects of futility, pain and love which did not apply to Suffolk and Norfolk's 1914–18 experience.

The Fixed Defences

by
Peter Kent

When Great Britain's ultimatum to Germany expired at midnight on 3 August 1914 and the Great War began, there were some of a nervous and imaginative disposition that expected the imminent arrival of the Kaiser's army on English beaches or, at the very least, the appearance of the High Seas Fleet to destroy every town that faced the North Sea. Since the 1890s when Admiral Tirpitz began to construct a fleet to rival the Royal Navy, fears of German intentions had increased with every new warship that hoisted the Imperial ensign. Throughout the nineteenth century periodic invasion scares had resulted in successive layers of fortifications that encrusted the major ports, but these had been sited on the assumption that the attackers would be French. After the *entente cordiale* in 1904 and Germany's rapid naval expansion, it had to be assumed that any invasion would be from across the North Sea rather than the Channel.

Strategic thinkers were united in their recognition of the German threat but divided as how to counter it. There was the Blue Water School which taught that so long as Britain retained command of the sea there was no possibility of invasion, and that the money the opposition advocated spending on fortifications and extra troops would be best spent on ships or not at all. Winston Churchill expressed the problem succinctly: 'As to a stronger regular army, either we had the command of the sea or we had not. If we had it we required fewer soldiers, if we had it not we wanted more ships.'[1] Fisher, the First Sea Lord, put it more forcefully: 'The Navy is the first, second, third, fourth, fifth . . . ad infinitum line of defence! If the Navy is not supreme, no army however large is of the slightest use. It's not *invasion* we have to fear if our Navy is beaten, IT'S STARVATION!'[2]

In 1905 the Government accepted the ideas of the Blue Water School and the Prime Minister Arthur Balfour made a speech in which he assured the country that, provided the Navy was efficient, 'serious invasion of these islands is not an eventuality which we need to seriously consider'.[3] Although a maximum invasion force of 70,000 men was envisaged, all detailed military plans assumed that an enemy would launch nothing more than minor raids of a couple of thousand troops with a few light guns, or rest content with bombarding coastal towns from cruisers. This did not,

1

however, stop leading military figures, of whom Lord Roberts was the most distinguished, from advocating conscription, or at the very least the introduction of rifle shooting as a national hobby. It also failed to halt the flood of books, plays and articles on the strategic implications and domestic consequences of German invasion.

Between 1901 and the outbreak of the Great War over forty full length novels on such a theme were published. It seemed that the public could not be given enough descriptions of enemy armies marching through the Home Counties to subject London to all the horrors of bombardment and pillage. Normally they were German but occasionally they featured interlopers from further afield: the Chinese on one occasion. The best seller was William Le Quex's *The Invasion of 1910* which within a few years of its publication in 1906 had sold over a million copies and been translated into twenty-seven languages. It described a German army landing suddenly at Lowestoft and then making its way to London by a curiously devious route, the ramifications of which were dictated more by the needs of the *Daily Mail*, which was serialising the book and liked headlines such as 'Kaiser at Saxmundham' and 'Prussians Storm Beccles', than those of realistic strategy. In *The Swoop of the Vulture* the Germans bombarded Lowestoft and Yarmouth, secret German sympathisers rose in revolt in *The Enemy in Our Midst*, while in *The Death Trap* the invading Teutons were only expelled by the timely intervention of the Japanese who landed at Liverpool. P. G. Wodehouse poked gentle fun at the whole genre in *The Swoop: Or, How Clarence Saved England: A Tale of the Great Invasion*. Clarence was a Boy Scout and single-handedly delivered the country from the combined massed forces of Germany, Russia, the Mad Mullah, the Young Turks and the Swiss Navy! Every year at least half a dozen books kept the idea of fleets of invasion barges packed with Prussian soldiery vividly alive. So when the much discussed war became uncomfortable reality it was hardly surprising that eyes turned seaward in almost hourly anticipation of sighting the top masts of the German High Seas Fleet and then turned to the shore to see what defences stood between England and the Kaiser's hordes.

There was nothing. Those who expected to see extensive fortifications and camps packed with troops were disappointed. Apart from the patrols of the Coastguard and the Boy Scouts, who had immediately volunteered their services to the War Office, the coast lay open and unprotected. Between the Wash and the Thames only Harwich had batteries with modern guns and was designated a fortress. Every other town was open to attack. King's Lynn possessed a small battery at the Coastguard station but its guns were only small quick-firers for training purposes. Wells, Blakeney, Sheringham and Cromer all stood completely unprotected. Yarmouth possessed an old battery on the South Denes with a few obsolete muzzle loaders, but this was as useless as an antique musket in modern war. Lowestoft had no defences at all and Southwold only its battery of six ancient and entirely ornamental cannon. Just south of Aldeburgh stood the last of a chain of Martello towers, but this was unarmed and derelict as were the others at Hollesley Bay and Felixstowe.

Felixstowe was part of the fortress of Harwich, which was a well-defended naval base sheltering a force of destroyers and light cruisers. The entrance to Harwich harbour was covered by the guns on either side, emplaced at Landguard Fort at Felixstowe and Beacon Hill Battery at Harwich. Landguard Fort was a mid-eighteenth century bastioned work, rebuilt in the 1870s with iron-shielded casemates, but those emplacements operational in 1914 lay outside the fort itself. These consisted of the right-flank battery with two six-inch guns (Plate I), and Darrell's Battery, named after the commander of the fort in 1667 who beat off a determined Dutch assault, which was armed with two 4·7-inch guns. Beacon Hill Battery was a modern work built in the 1890s, armed with two six-inch and two 4·7-inch guns, and

Imperial War Museum

Plate I. A Mark VII 6-inch gun in the Right Flank Battery, Landguard Fort

in Harwich itself there was the Redoubt, a circular Napoleonic work on the top of which were two 12-pounders. The harbour defences also included searchlights and a minefield. This efficient, but by no means formidable, armament was in the process of being supplemented by two modern 9·2-inch guns, for which emplacements were under construction at North Felixstowe[4] (Figure 1).

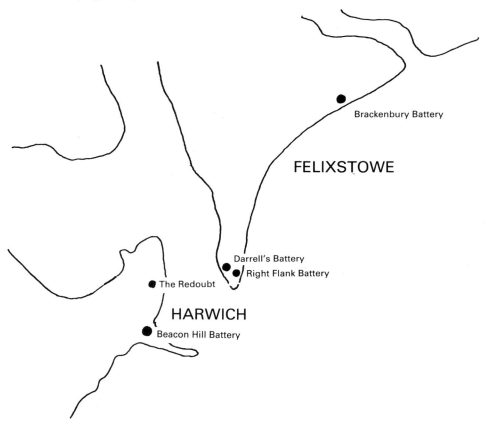

Figure 1. The defences of Harwich; 1914–18

From Harwich southwards the coast was without any defences apart from the abandoned Martello towers until the mouth of the Thames, where there was the Coast Artillery School and experimental range at Shoeburyness. Here, apart from the menagerie of experimental ordnance of varying degrees of efficiency, there were three batteries of modern guns used for training the coast gunners: one 9·2-inch, two 6-inch and two 4·7-inch and a number of 12- and 6-pounders (Plate II). Further upstream towards London

Major Tony Hill

Plate II.
A Mark X 9·2-inch gun at the Coast Artillery School, Shoeburyness

there were a number of large and elaborate fortifications, each representative of its era (Figure 2). At East Tilbury there was a large battery dating from the 1890s, at Coalhouse Point a great casemated fort of the 1860s and 70s and at West Tilbury a huge seventeenth-century bastioned fort. Ten years earlier, these had been armed with over 20 modern breech-loading guns but by the outbreak of the war these had been reduced to the four at Coalhouse Fort, because the increased range of artillery meant that the heavy guns were placed to better advantage further out in the estuary; by 1914, therefore, they were mounted at Sheerness and on the Isle of Grain. Another reason for the gradual reduction in armament, which affected Harwich as well as the Thames, was the anticipated small scale of any attack, despite the growth of German naval power. The only attack expected on Harwich was a raid by a couple of armoured cruisers, although with the installation of an Admiralty fuel store there in 1912 and the mooring of a floating dock, the harbour's protection was upgraded by the authorisation of the 9·2-inch battery at North Felixstowe.[5]

The extreme advocates of the Blue Water School would have removed every gun and even the Boy Scouts from the coast, but all but the most committed exponents of naval supremacy in matters of national defence

5

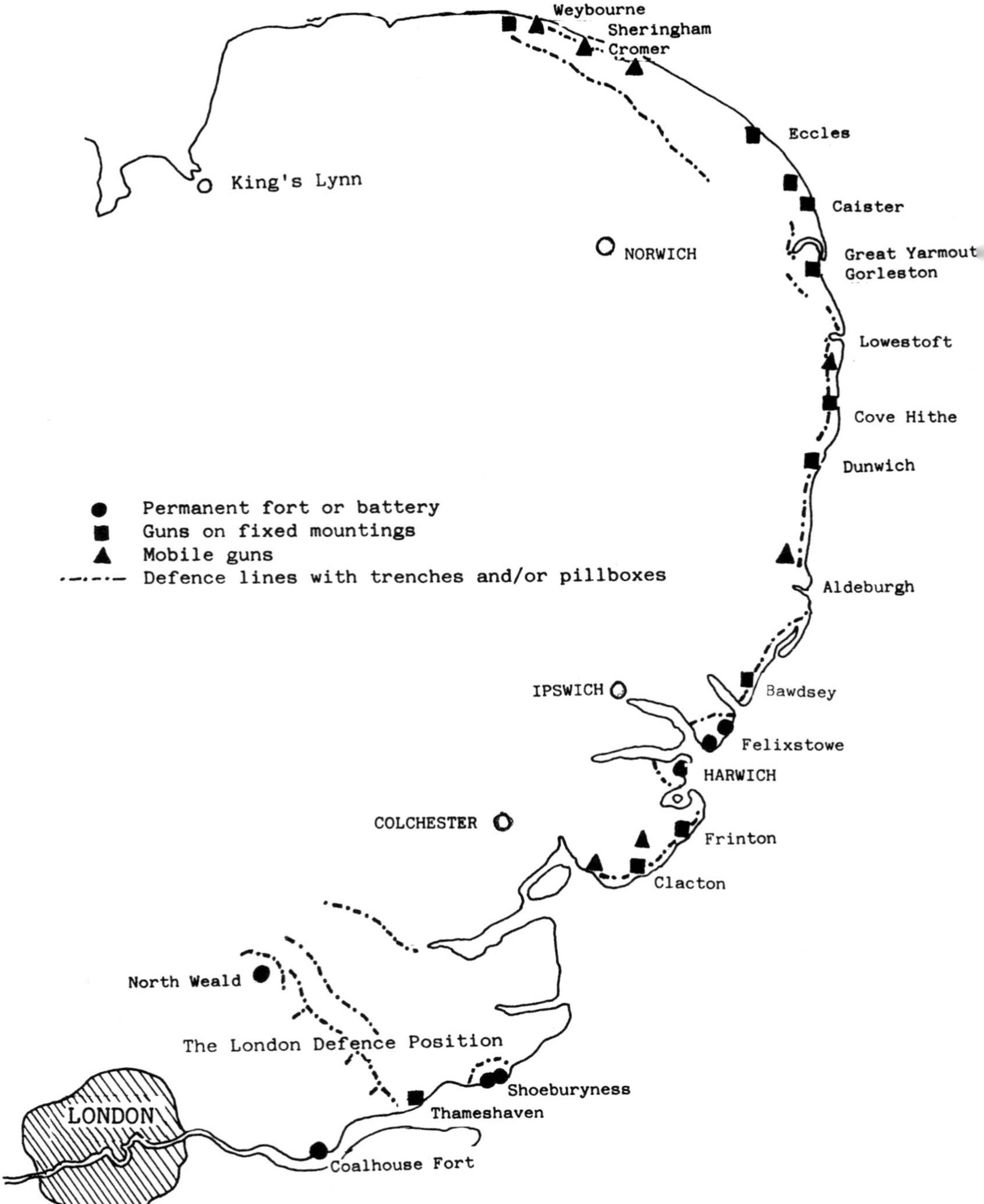
Weybourne
Sheringham
Cromer
Eccles
King's Lynn
Caister
NORWICH
Great Yarmout
Gorleston
Lowestoft
Cove Hithe
Dunwich
Permanent fort or battery
Guns on fixed mountings
Mobile guns
Defence lines with trenches and/or pillboxes
Aldeburgh
IPSWICH
Bawdsey
Felixstowe
HARWICH
COLCHESTER
Frinton
Clacton
North Weald
The London Defence Position
Shoeburyness
Thameshaven
LONDON
Coalhouse Fort

Figure 2. The Defences of East Anglia, 1914–18

allowed for some second line of resistance. It was always possible that a raid might be mounted to cause alarm and disruption and a few fast steamers might slip across the North Sea at night to land several thousand men on the East Anglian coast. The arrival of the Grand Fleet would have soon cut off their escape, and the damage would have been negligible except in political terms, but this was enough to prompt measures to counter it. In case the Germans should have been so foolish as to attempt such an adventure, plans drawn up for the land defence of the eastern counties were implemented. Each of the three counties of Essex, Norfolk and Suffolk was defended by one Infantry Brigade, one mounted Yeomanry Brigade, a brigade of the Royal Field Artillery and two battalions of cyclists. In addition to this field force, Harwich Fortress had a garrison of six battalions of infantry.[6] Although on paper these dispositions looked neatly symmetrical the tactical arrangements were rather different.

Because large stretches of the coast – the shores of the Wash, the salt-marshes west of Weybourne, Orford Ness and Foulness Island – remained invulnerable to any landing in strength due to the difficulty of getting inland quickly, troops were concentrated at the most likely landing places. In all cases these were the same as in previous invasion scares: the north Norfolk coast between Cley and Sheringham, the open beaches south of Lowestoft and the stretch of coast between Walton on the Naze and the mouth of the River Colne. Once the troops were in place all that remained to do was to dig the defences, but in the summer of 1914 this was delayed: partly because the war was expected to be short, and also from a desire not to alarm the holidaymakers who were still on the beaches.[7] As the war dragged on into the autumn and winter the fortification of the coast began in earnest, given priority by an event that many had long feared: the German fleet emerged from its fortified bases, dashed across the North Sea and bombarded Yarmouth and Lowestoft on 3 November. Damage was slight, the heavy armour-piercing shells with their small bursting charge of high-explosive proving almost useless against buildings, and the incident proved the futility of such actions in a military sense; but the outcry kept the fear of invasion in the forefront of the public mind, and stimulated further trench-digging. Sheringham Golf Links were desecrated by a complex trench system that extended as far as Weybourne, and further trenches to form reserve lines of defence were dug between Hunworth and Briston[8] (Figure 2); by the following year there were six 4·7-inch guns on travelling carriages at Weybourne and a further two at Cromer.[9]

In case the enemy should land, and even more improbably if they should begin to advance on London, a series of defence lines were plannd to run north of the capital to bar the way of an invading force advancing from either Norfolk or Essex. Since the 1880s the possibility of a force advancing from the east coast had been countered by proposals to build defensive lines at Epping and Brentwood where all routes from the east converged. The plans were put into operation in 1915; called the London Defence Position, the works followed the prepared line from Epping to the Thames, with an outer position at Brentwood and later a third line running from Chelmsford to Maldon[10] (Figure 2). This system of field fortifications included the only permanent land fort in East Anglia, the North Weald Redoubt, which was completed in 1890. It was not a massive concrete affair with deep ditches, extensive casemates and armoured cupolas, like the Belgian forts which had been pulverised the previous year, but a mainly earthwork redoubt with some casemated accommodation and magazines. It was not intended to be the main defence of the position, but more a permanent strongpoint around which fieldworks could be constructed in an emergency, serving in peace time as a store for the equipment needed to complete the rest of the defences.[11]

Harwich was made into a self-contained fortress immediately war was declared by constructing a defensive perimeter of trenches and barbed wire that cut off the peninsula to the west of Parkestone Quay.[12] On the Felixstowe side of the harbour the defences mainly occupied the heights at Walton so that Landguard Fort and its batteries could not be bombarded from the rear, although there were additional outposts to defend the new battery at North Felixstowe, which was hurriedly completed in 1915 and named after General Brackenbury, a former Director of Military Intelligence. It mounted two 9·2-inch Mk X guns which had been brought from Berehaven on the west coast of Ireland. These were the most powerful artillery pieces ever to be emplaced on the East Anglian coast, capable of firing a 280-pound shell to 17,000 yards and quite able to deal with any German ship that might have the temerity to bombard Harwich.[13]

To meet the less likely threat of a landing on the shores of the Thames estuary, a force of infantry, artillery and cavalry was deployed, supported by field fortifications. These works were mainly located at Shoeburyness, comprising an extensive system of trenches, barbed wire entanglements, blockhouses and pillboxes. The blockhouses were similar to those used in the South African War and probably made from components held in store, they were simple constructions of two circular corrugated iron walls set about two feet apart with the intervening space filled with sand and gravel.[14]

The most unusual addition to the defence that year was the armoured train stationed in Norfolk, employed to give an element of mobility (Plate III). Its use was rather more reassuring than practical for although an armoured train combined all the mystique of the railway with the panoply of warfare it was not really an effective weapon. 'Nothing looks more formidable and impressive than an armoured train; but nothing is in fact more vulnerable and helpless.'[15] All the enemy had to do was to blow up a culvert or simply

National Railway Museum

Plate III. Armoured Train, Number One, fresh out of the workshops at Crewe

remove a rail and the train was immobilised, and if the enemy was not so obliging as to have remained within range then all the train's armament was useless. But despite these objections the War Office decided to provide two trains for those remote and vulnerable areas of the coast that were served by railways: one was stationed in Scotland, the other at North Walsham. It was made up of four wagons and an engine, all converted from commercial stock, the armour-plated locomotive, a Great Northern Railway tank engine, located in the middle of the train. On either side was a long van, loopholed and plated in half-inch steel, with accommodation for the crew, and at either end of the train a gun truck with a Maxim machine gun and a 12-pounder naval gun. The train clanked impressively up and down the Mundesley branch line and as far afield as Yarmouth until it was withdrawn at the end of the war without ever firing a shot.[16]

Despite these sometimes ingenious arrangements to combat invasion from the sea, the main enemy assault on England came from a novel quarter: the air. What had been fancifully predicted in pre-war fiction became reality when a Zeppelin dropped a bomb in Whitehall Yard, Sheringham, in January 1915, giving it the uncomfortable distinction of the first place in Britain to be so attacked. The stretch of coast between Happisburgh and Hunstanton was regularly crossed by Zeppelins on their way inland and anti-aircraft defences were hurriedly improvised and sent to Norfolk. The first anti-aircraft guns were mobile and under control of the Navy. The R.N. Mobile Brigade was stationed in Norfolk for most of 1916 and equipped with four 75-mm, two 3-inch and eight 3-pounder lorry-mounted guns, with three mobile searchlights.[17] As the Zeppelins used the Happisburgh lightship as a navigation aid, two of the 75-mm guns were stationed in a sandbagged emplacement at Bacton and were in action on several occasions, without ever destroying a Zeppelin. Although guns were in short supply and vital military targets in need of protection were many, the remaining two 75-mm guns were sent to protect Sandringham House where Queen Alexandra had taken up residence.[18] The R.N. Brigade was withdrawn to Essex in 1917 but replaced in Norfolk by an Army Brigade of three mobile batteries armed with 13-pounders, another brigade with eighteen 13-pounders being based at Harwich.[19] The guns were dispersed over a wide area and rarely stayed in the same village for more than a few days. In addition to the nomadic mobile guns, static artillery was emplaced at important points: the British airship base at Pulham Market was covered by three 3-inch, Yarmouth had two 18-pounders and a line of gun stations was established to the east of London to deal with Zeppelins and aircraft navigating by the line of the Thames.[20] To supplement the London guns, every new Army mobile battery was sent to the north east of London to complete training before being sent to France.[21] It was the guns on the parade ground of Tilbury Fort that scored the only success of the ground forces against the Zeppelins: they so damaged L 15 that it later sank into the sea off the Kent coast.

In 1916 there was a renewed fear of German invasion and a consequent strengthening of the land defences. These fears were compounded in April of that year when Lowestoft was bombarded for the second time by the High Seas Fleet, an event which caused widespread panic, people fleeing inland as far as Bungay; for weeks afterwards every barn and shed for miles around was full of townspeople who trekked out into the country to sleep.[22] The report of the incident in the local press made no reference to the alarm and was a masterpiece of laconic understatement: 'Lowestoft had a very trying experience on Tuesday morning, the bombardment of the town by a powerful German cruiser squadron.'[23] The response to this assault was to dig more trenches along the cliffs at Pakefield, which were duly inspected by the King, and to moor two shallow-draught monitors in the Hamilton Dock: H.M.S. *Glowworm*, armed with two 6-inch guns, and her larger companion H.M.S. *Havelock* with two 14-inch and two 6-inch guns. The 2/1st Essex Heavy Battery, Royal Garrison Artillery, armed with six 60-pounders, was stationed in Lowestoft and regularly fired its guns in practise from Pakefield cliffs.[24]

A joint meeting of the Admiralty and War Office in January came to the conclusion that the Germans, despite the fact that their fleet lay idle in harbour and that their armies were fully engaged on two fronts, might make a force of ten divisions, or 160,000 men, available for an invasion of England. If they slipped across by night the British Grand Fleet could not intervene for twenty-four hours, by which time all the enemy troops and sufficient artillery would have landed.[25] In August, after the Battle of Jutland, there was a further meeting which came to the same alarmist conclusion. Despite the entire German battle cruiser squadron being out of action, the Grand Fleet in indisputed command of the sea, and the German Army suffering huge losses at Verdun, it was still thought possible for the Germans to get 160,000 men across the North Sea and land them on English beaches without their being seriously hampered or molested.[26] To deal with the potential threat of invasion, the General Staff decided that a minimum of half a million troops were required at all times in the United Kingdom. Just over half of these were to be mobile and capable of counter offensives, while the remaining 230,000 were to be made up of base units, coast artillery and other sedentary and garrison troops. There were six divisions of infantry available, twelve yeomanry brigades and a number of cyclist battalions, of which all but one infantry division were stationed in the south east. If the Germans were to land anywhere, the General Staff surmised, it would be between the Wash and Dover; but as there was a new battle squadron stationed in the Thames, consisting of one dreadnought and five of the most modern pre-dreadnoughts, it was thought most likely that the enemy would land further north. The Wash itself was ruled out: 'A landing on the shores of the Wash itself of anything but a very small force is extremely improbable.'[27] North Norfolk was considered more probable but still unlikely, the General Staff's prediction being that it was Suffolk that would see the first Germans wading through the surf. 'The most favourable stretch of coast for the landing of the expedition is considered to be that between Aldeburgh and Lowestoft.'[28]

It was according to this supposition that the defences were arranged. The five infantry divisions available in the south east were arranged in two armies, the northern with its H.Q. at Lynford Hall near Mundford and the southern with its H.Q. at Brentford. The northern army had two infantry divisions, one cyclist division, four provisional brigades of infantry and four attached battalions of cyclists; in addition a reserve division was available in case of invasion, stationed at Bedford. The southern army was responsible for both north and south of the Thames, its forces made up of three infantry divisions, one cyclist division with four attached battalions, six provisional brigades and the 1st Mounted Division. With four battalions to a brigade and three brigades to a division this meant a total of 112 battalions of infantry, thirty-two battalions of cyclists and nine regiments of cavalry; or about 140,000 infantry and 4,000 cavalry with artillery and other arms. The basic plan was to hold the coastline with provisional battalions fighting from trenches, and if the invaders should penetrate inland, which the General Staff thought inevitable, for it was 'quite impossible to ensure that the enemy will meet with serious resistance at the landing places he may select for his disembarkation',[29] then they would be met with vigorous counter-strokes from the mobile forces. If this failed then there were the field fortifications of the London Position, manned by fifty-three battalions of infantry. Unlike the Second World War, when there was both a strong coastal crust of defences and successive stoplines inland, the policy of the Great War was to have a coastal defence and then nothing until the London Position at Chelmsford. This was because it was assumed that any German invasion would not be an attempt to capture the whole country but simply a direct blow at London to achieve a quick end to the war.

Although the coastal fortifications of the Great War never approached the scale of those of either the Napoleonic or Second World War, they were by 1917 quite substantial. Most of the coast from the Wash to the Thames was entrenched in those places where it was judged practicable for an enemy to land: there were trench systems at Weybourne and Sheringham, Sea Palling and around Yarmouth; Lowestoft and the coast southwards of Aldeburgh was heavily defended and there were more trenches at Bawdsey. Harwich and Felixstowe formed a self-contained fortress and the rest of the coast to the mouth of the Thames was lightly defended except for the stretch between Walton on the Naze and Clacton. Apart from the permanent coastal batteries on the Thames and around Harwich there were comparatively few guns actually emplaced along the coast, although the mobile artillery of the defending armies would be available if the situation made it necessary.

There were heavy batteries of the Royal Garrison Artillery each armed with six 60-pounders or 4·7-inch guns at Weybourne, Mundesley, Pakefield, Leiston, Thorpe Le Soken and St. Osyth.[30] Although these were field guns and of no use against armoured or even moving ships, they would have been dangerous to anchored transports unloading troops. In addition to these mobile guns, there were two 4·7-inch at Cromer, and a single 4·7-inch naval gun in an entrenchment on Gorleston cliffs; two 15-pounders at Salthouse and Dunwich, one 15-pounder at Eccles, Newport, Caister, Cove Hithe, and Thorpeness, and four 15-pounders at Bawdsey, Clacton and Frinton. Then there were no emplaced weapons at all until Shoeburyness and further up the Thames two 12-pounders at Thameshaven, and the two remaining 6-inch guns at Coalhouse Fort.[31] Combined with the monitors stationed at

Peter Kent

Plate IV. Circular pillbox at Bradfield, near North Walsham

13

Plate V. Hexagonal pillbox at Haddiscoe still fulfilling a useful function

Lowestoft and Yarmouth, these guns comprised a coastal armament capable of at the least seriously inconveniencing an enemy attempting to land; in those days before purpose-built front-loading landing craft the whole process of disembarking an army was a much slower and more exposed business.[32]

To support the trenchlines concrete pillboxes were built from 1917 to the end of the war. The British first encountered them on the Western Front where they formed formidable additions to the German trench systems, and engineers were quick to realise their usefulness. Three basic types were constructed in East Anglia, most of which survived to be reincorporated in the defence lines of the Second World War. In North Norfolk a long line was built slightly inland from Weybourne to Sea Palling, most of these along the line of the River Ant and defending every crossing to The Waybridge near Stalham. They were circular, made of concrete blocks,

14

with steel shuttered loopholes and steel doors (Plate IV). A second type, sited near Yarmouth, was the prototype of the common hexagonal standard pillbox of the Second World War; about 18 inches thick, built of poured reinforced concrete with steel-lined loopholes and half-inch thick doors, two of these still survive on either side of the Acle New Road outside Yarmouth and there is another at Haddiscoe (Plate V). Facing towards the east, their purpose was to contain an invading force that had already landed, many being built to the south of Lowestoft, and two on the cliffs at Corton. Those at Lowestoft were built in April and May 1918 at the height of the German offensive, suggesting that the General Staff thought that the Germans might make a last desperate effort to resolve matters by landing a force in England, a theory supported by the Army's rehearsal of procedures to combat a landing as late as June 1918. The third type was circular, without loopholes and steel doors, and several of these survive at Bawdsey and Hollesley Bay. Small, squat and circular with a slightly overhanging roof, all they need is a label to be almost perfect replicas of their namesakes (Plate VI).

None of these defences ever fired at a German ship and when the war ended in November 1918 the whole extensive system was rapidly dismantled. All the guns, except those in the permanent batteries, were removed and the trench systems filled in. All that remained was the few dozen pillboxes, abandoned until the next war.

Peter Kent

Plate VI. A circular pillbox at Bawdsey

Notes

1. Quoted in Dunlop, J. K. Col., *The Development of the British Army, 1899–1914* (London, 1938), pp. 156–58.
2. Quoted in Marder, A. J., *The Anatomy of British Sea Power; A History of British Naval Policy in the Pre-Dreadnought Era, 1880–1905* (London, 1964), p. 65.
3. Ibid., p. 81.
4. P.R.O. CAB/12/1.
5. P.R.O. CAB/17/109.
6. P.R.O. WO/153/425.
7. Hankey, Lord, *The Supreme Command* (London, 1961), ii, p. 215.
8. Cambell Erroll, A., *A History of Sheringham and Beeston Regis* (Norwich, 1970), p. 74.
9. P.R.O. WO/33/828.
10. The defence lines were based on the plans set out in the *Handbook for the London Position* (War Office, 1903): see also Smith, V. C., 'The Changing Face of English Fortifications, 1870–1918', *Post Medieval Archaeology*, XIX (1985), p. 143.
11. P.R.O. WO/78/2606.
12. P.R.O. WO/78/4423.
13. P.R.O. WO/192/205.
14. P.R.O. WO/78/4410.
15. Churchill, W. S., *My Early Life* (London, 1958), p. 167.
16. Balfour, G., *The Armoured Train; Its Development and Usage* (London, 1981).
17. Rawlinson, A., *The Defence of London, 1915–1918* (London, 1923), p. 150.
18. Ibid., pp. 95–96.
19. P.R.O. WO/33/828.
20. Ibid.
21. Hogg, I. V., *Anti-Aircraft; A History of Air Defence* (London, 1978), p. 49.
22. Bignold, R. Canon, *The Chronicles of Carlton Colville* (Lowestoft, 1982), p. 12.
23. *Norwich Mercury*, 29 April 1916, p. 3.
24. P.R.O. WO/33/779(6).
25. P.R.O. WO/33/771.
26. Ibid.
27. P.R.O. WO/33/872.
28. Ibid.
29. P.R.O. WO/33/871.
30. P.R.O. WO/33/779.

31. P.R.O. WO/33/828.
32. An experiment had been carried out off Clacton in 1904 to determine how rapidly an invasion force could disembark. Twelve thousand men, 2,500 horses, fifty-five guns and 320 vehicles were landed from ten ships in twenty hours. As this was a peacetime exercise it was realised a landing in wartime conditions would be faster. It was also assumed that if the Germans sent a large force they could not all land on one beach. A force of 120,000 men carried in two hundred ships anchored in three lines would need ten to thirteen miles of open beach to disembark. As there was not a single stretch of beach of that length from the Wash to the Thames it was obvious that an invading force would land at several places; hence the need to keep the arrangements for counter-attacks as fluid as possible (P.R.O. WO/33/771).

Volunteers and Recruiting

by

Nicholas Mansfield

Military Traditions in East Anglia

During the nineteenth century many young men from East Anglian parishes, if they were in trouble with the law through poaching or illegitimate children, joined the army. Large impoverished families, especially in times of agricultural depression, acted as further inducements to enlist. They usually served in the Norfolk or Suffolk Regiments. Once in the forces, they would mix with men from Scotland, Ireland and the industrial areas, who made up the majority of the army. Subject to fierce discipline, they would, if lucky, return to follow the plough in their home parishes with a small pension. Except perhaps during the Napoleonic Wars, when military service was more widespread, it was a disgrace in respectable working class families to have a son serving as a private soldier. Often ex-soldiers were discriminated against in employment. In his autobiography *Crowscaring to Westminster*, George Edwards, the founder of the farm-workers' union, tells of his father Thomas, who had served ten years in the 60th Rifles. In the 1830s he was paid 1s. a week less than other labourers and forced to work a seven day week. This low wage led his family in a downward spiral that ended in prison and the workhouse.

Even the Cardwell reforms did not alter this discrimination, as Rider Haggard outlined:

'(soldiers) almost invariably return after their eight years service to find themselves absolutely unfitted at six-and-twenty or so to follow the vocation of an agricultural labourer. A few get situations as grooms . . . but there is a general, though frequently a very unjust, prejudice against them. The farmers will have nothing to do with them, for they say, perhaps rightly that they have lost touch with the land, and are of little use upon it . . . The worst thing that a young fellow from a county village can do is enlist, unless he means to make soldiering the profession of his life.'[1]

Until the Boer War, military service was not popular with East Anglians, although the establishment of the Territorial Force in 1908 made part-time soldiering more respectable. Nevertheless it is interesting to see how the

18

traditional view of the army underlay recruiting well into the Great War.

The territorials themselves were recruited from a cross section of society. The Cambridgeshire Regiment was a good example of this:

'. . . the four Cambridge Companies comprised college servants, printers from the Pitt Press, gas workers, clerks, shop assistants, in fact a sprinkling of all that goes to make up the population of a University town. The other four Companies recruiting from the Isle of Ely were mainly agricultural – smallholders and agricultural labourers, and a good number of railway workers. As a subaltern I commanded "E" Company, drawn from Wisbech – timber sawyers, solicitors' clerks, men drawn from fruit orchards, a large proportion of the local Post Office staff, in short men from all trades.'[2]

The battalion was 960 strong and in August 1914 had a waiting list of men wishing to join.

The Kitchener Appeal

Whilst most generals and politicians considered that the war would be over by Christmas, Lord Kitchener foresaw a long struggle and appealed for 100,000 men to create a 'New Army' to make good losses already sustained in France. Kitchener's posters began to be put up in Cambridgeshire on 10 August, and recruiting offices were opened in Norfolk in the second week of August 1914. Often these were in private houses. Mrs Townshend, wife of General Townshend, enlisted men at Vere Lodge, Raynham, and Major J. H. Kennedy, a retired army officer, opened his house at Attleborough.

For the first few months of recruiting the flavour of semi-official private armies was sustained. The County Territorial Associations which controlled the pre-war Territorial Force could not cope. Norfolk was divided into four areas, but the queues of recruits seen in other parts of the country did not materialise. At the beginning of September only 350 men had volunteered for the New Army in the southern recruiting area of the county. (This does not include those who joined the Territorials.) Harvest was consuming the energies of the farming community, and the international crisis had to wait. The *Norfolk News* announced on 22 August: 'When the harvest is over, however, it is confidently expected that the number of enlistments will be considerably larger.'

Billy Dixon, a farmworker from Trunch: 'When the war came out, just as we started harvest . . . and so I joined up as soon as we finished harvest . . . They were calling out for volunteers them days. Several of us in the village, I should think about ten of us, went that day to Mundesley and took the shilling.'[3]

Another reason for the slow recruiting was the physical difficulty in large rural areas of actually finding somewhere to enlist. Many men who had to walk long distances to recruiting offices were deterred. Harry Smith, an eighteen year old builder's labourer, walked six miles to Wymondham in September 1914, on hearing the rumour of a recruiting officer in the town. Unable to enlist, and discouraged, he went home and finished the building job on which he was engaged. When this ended in November, he walked to Britannia Barracks in Norwich and enlisted there.

Even in a town as large as Cambridge there could be difficulties in enlisting, particularly as there was no regular county regiment. The local territorials were over-subscribed and no Kitchener battalion was formed there until the end of September. Consequently men such as Sam Fairweather walked, with a group of fellow railwaymen, the twenty-seven miles to the Suffolks' depot, Gibraltar Barracks at Bury St Edmunds. (In Fairweather's case this was a fruitless journey – he was rejected as being too old at 34, and too useful in his present occupation.)

In Norfolk, when both the first and second line territorials were filled up, potential recruits were told to go home. Although the local press printed a retraction of this statement, it caused considerable confusion, and underlined the inefficiency of the County Territorial Associations. One recruit was reported as saying: 'I've been up to Norwich twice already on this business not knowing each time whether I should return home.'[4]

On 5 September the *Norfolk News* announced: 'With the finish of harvest work the Norfolk labourers are rapidly making their way to the recruiting stations.' On that day, 230 men had enlisted at Dereham, 100 at Fakenham, 19 at Hempton Fair, no doubt persuaded in the time honoured way by recruiting sergeants with ribbons in their hats!

During the following week 3,000 Norfolk recruits had been gathered together at Norwich, including a businessmen's company formed from the business houses of the city. Another 3,000 were collected together at Dereham for training. With shortages of all materials they were formed in huge temporary battalions of 1,300–1,400 men. They were a cross section of Norfolk society with farm labourers and 'gentleman ranker', and as such represented a much higher standard of recruit in health, education and abilities, than pre-war recruits for the regular army. Many of them were under age. Billy Dixon of Trunch, again: 'You had to be twenty-one them days. When I went up they said, "You aren't twenty yet." "All right," I say, "I'm twenty-one." Some weren't about sixteen, seventeen.'

Firms such as Colmans made declarations that they would pay a separation allowance of five shillings a week for each recruit's wife and up to ten shillings for a couple with five children. At the Norfolk Chamber of Agriculture it was reported that: 'It has been suggested that it would inspire greater confidence among labourers who are likely to enlist if they were sure that their places would be kept open for them on their return from the war.'[5] A list of farmers willing to do so was compiled; how many kept their word is unknown.

Motivation

The war was greeted with genuine enthusiasm, and patriotism was a clear motive for many in joining up. Propaganda on behalf of the Empire had been taught in schools and intensified since the Boer War. The violation of Belgian neutrality seemed a good cause. Britain seemed to have a logical set of war aims, and these seemed to unite much of society in a way which we have seen in our own times in the Falklands War. German militarism and fear of invasion was stressed by propaganda from the beginning. Bill Curtis of Salhouse recalls that: 'They said Kaiser Bill was coming with his men and all the youngsters went.'[6]

Many East Anglian people did not travel, and the war seemed a good way of having an exciting, expenses paid holiday away from the boredom of work. Male bonding groups reinforced this trend. Clubs, groups of work mates, football teams, Sunday School classes, friendly society lodges, all joined together, not wanting to be left out. An undertaking was made that groups of friends who enlisted together would be kept together in the same unit. At the beginning of September, Major Besant announced at a recruiting meeting in Norwich: 'Various groups will remain together as comrades throughout the whole of their service. Such a provision will enable men of any class whatever to enlist with the knowledge that they will have congenial company.' Later that month at North Walsham, Major Pearce addressed a parade of his 120 recruits: 'I have made a special request that you should be enrolled and go to Norwich together and serve together.' This was to have awful repercussions two years later on the Somme.

There was an element of compulsion from the early days of the war. Some women exerted pressure on men, even before the white feather campaign began, to create a climate in which men felt it was their duty to go. To encourage the momentum of recruiting, meetings held throughout the area were addressed by public figures, and by representatives of all political parties. The Labour Party in Norwich, forgetting its pre-war pacifism, joined in this. Fred Henderson, a fiery socialist who served a prison sentence in 1889 for his part in an unemployment riot declared that: 'Coltishall might share the fate as Dinant.'[7]

These meetings, and the worries of those presiding, were reported extensively in the local press. E. G. Hemmerde, a Liberal M.P., was reported as saying in Hunstanton on 12 September: 'Now that the harvest was practically gathered in there was a lot of first rate fellows in Norfolk who ought to be fighting.' During the same week, the Earl of Leicester told a meeting in the Oddfellows Hall at Wells: 'Some parishes had not yet come forward as they should have done.' Often the numbers volunteering after these meetings were reported, but sometimes they are given as 'several', 'a number' or 'a few more'.

It is important not to ignore the traditional motive of poverty, particularly in large families, increased by the economic dislocation brought on by the war crisis. George Howell of Walsingham commented: 'I went into the forces – like a fool! I was, I was a young fool. The reason why I joined the army was to get my feet out from under the table, so there was four or five there to be fed. My eldest sister had to go into service.'[8] Other young men enlisted with confused motives, drifting in after harvest, bored with many of their friends gone.

Even at this stage of the war there was a certain amount of opposition from families when their sons wanted to go. Usually this was on traditional lines. Harry Smith of Eccles said: 'The Army was mud to my people . . . Well, they tried all ways to persuade me not to – my mother especially, of course.'[9] By late September the pace of recruiting had slackened. Despite all the pressures on single young men, the Rector of Burnham Thorpe could still write of his village: 'I know that there are a dozen fellows who might join and do not.'[10]

Military Structure
The structure of military recruiting was very complicated and is best explained in relation to one county. Before 1914 most Norfolk soldiers served in the Regular battalions (1st and 2nd) of the Norfolk Regiment. As there was a cavalry barracks at Pockthorpe in Norwich, certain mounted units recruited locally whilst stationed there. Some Norfolk men served in artillery, engineer and other ancillary units, and even other infantry units of the army. As the war progressed and most of the pre-war regulars became casualties, these regular units were filled up with volunteers and, after 1916, with conscripts. They still thought of themselves as regulars and maintained 'regular' standards of discipline.

The 3rd Battalion was a remnant of the old militia battalion and consisted of a training cadre of officers and sergeants. Thousands of Norfolk men did their training in its ranks.

The 4th, 5th and 6th Battalions and the Norfolk Yeomanry were territorials; part-time soldiers. They were mobilised at the beginning of the war, and most volunteered for foreign service. (About 70% of the 4th Norfolks volunteered.) However, overseas service was not universally popular among territorials who had joined for home service only. Few went so far as Private Harry Hook of Elveden, a member of the Suffolk Yeomanry, who committed suicide on receiving orders to go abroad, but a solution had to be found to incorporate these men. Territorial battalions were each ordered to raise an additional 'second line' battalion from the influx of volunteers and from men not willing to go abroad. These second line battalions were intended as home service units, but increasingly they were sent on active service. After the introduction of conscription, those who still refused to volunteer overseas were sometimes brought before

Norfolk Military Structure (simplified)

1st Battalion	Norfolk Regiment		Regulars
2nd Battalion	Norfolk Regiment		
Cavalry, Artillery, Engineers, etc.			
3rd Battalion	Norfolk Regiment	(Training Battalion) ex-militia	Special Reserve
		'2nd line Territorials'	
1/4 Battalion	Norfolk Regiment	2/4th	
1/5 Battalion	Norfolk Regiment	2/5th	Territorials
1/6 Battalion	Norfolk Regiment	(Cyclists) 2/6th	
7th Battalion	Norfolk Regiment	Service Battalion	
8th Battalion	Norfolk Regiment	Service Battalion	
9th Battalion	Norfolk Regiment	Service Battalion	New Army
10th Battalion	Norfolk Regiment	Training Battalion	
Norfolk Yeomanry	(Later 12th Norfolks)		

military tribunals and pressured to serve. In March 1916 a farmer's son was dismissed from the Norfolk Yeomanry and presumably later conscripted. This was not always the case. When, in 1916, Lord Hastings, a non-overseas volunteer, was promoted to command the 2nd Norfolk Yeomanry, a public outcry resulted in questions in the House of Commons. But Hastings retained his command. It proved difficult to keep up the numbers of territorial volunteers after the initial inrush, and by the end of the war 'second line' territorial divisions were contemptuously referred to as 'conscript divisions' by generals. It could take some time to send even the first line territorials abroad. A crack unit such as the 1st Cambridgeshires (the premier county battalion), did not reach France until February 1915.

The 7th, 8th, 9th and 10th Service Battalions of the Norfolk Regiment were the Norfolk element of Kitchener's New Army, and were the units created from the mass of Norfolk volunteers in 1914. All except the 10th, which was a training unit, were operational battalions on the Western Front. There was no attempt to form a City of Norwich battalion. The service battalions drew their recruits from all over the county, although the 8th Battalion is sometimes referred to as the Businessmen's Battalion, because of its company of Norwich clerks. The same pattern was repeated in Suffolk and Cambridgeshire with the raising of the 7th, 8th, 9th Suffolks, the 11th Suffolks (the Cambridge battalion), and the 12th Suffolks, a Bantam battalion for men too short for the normal regulation height, which drew recruits from the whole of East Anglia.

Other Norfolk volunteers served in many other units of the British Army, and this trend was intensified after conscription was introduced. East

23

Anglians also served in the Australian and Canadian contingents. These were mostly emigrants, but the Canadian government had a recruiting office in Liverpool. Men that had relations in Canada were eligible to join and so got the superior pay, conditions and uniforms of the Canadians. (Sixty-five per cent of the rank and file of the first Canadian contingent had been born in Britain.) Dominion troops (all volunteers), later became the 'shock' troops of the Imperial army. Amounting to one-sixth of the total British Empire strength, they were given difficult tasks in battle.

As a maritime county, many Norfolk men served in the Navy. Fishing fleets at Lynn and Yarmouth were transformed into the Royal Navy Volunteers Reserve to act as minesweepers. When the great naval battles did not materialise, Norfolk sailors served alongside Norfolk's soldiers, on the Western Front as members of the Royal Naval Division.

The Norfolk Yeomanry was an interesting county institution. A cavalry regiment, formed originally during the Napoleonic Wars, they continued their existence as part-time troops, ready to be called out in case of riots. (They served, for example, in the anti-workhouse riots at Docking in 1834.) They were revived as an Imperial institution at the time of the Boer War, and consisted mostly of men from the hunting fraternity. The masters of the West Norfolk Foxhounds and the Norwich Staghounds were always among the officers. Members of the aristocracy, like Lord Hastings, served as captains, large farmers were N.C.O.s and sons of tenant farmers made up most of the troopers. Prince Duleep Singh, an exile from the Punjab who lived at Elveden Hall, became an honorary Englishman, and served as a major. A 2nd Norfolk Yeomanry was raised for home service, while the 1st fought in Gallipoli, the Middle East and France. It suffered the indignity of losing its horses, and being converted to infantry as the 12th Battalion Norfolk Regiment. However, members of the battalion still thought of themselves as Yeomen and illegally retained their cap badges.

Training

Most volunteers regarded themselves as civilians in uniform. The large numbers of surviving photographs, often with self-deprecatory comments, testifies to this. When it seemed that the war would be over by Christmas, many expected that they would merely be doing a little light garrison duty. The acute shortages of all equipment that existed among the early volunteer formations perpetuated this dressing-up feeling and the billeting of men in tents added to the holiday atmosphere. Sixty recruits at the Cambridge Corn Exchange were told to go home as the organisation could not cope with them. This, these young working class men refused to do since they had given up their jobs and had no means of support. They slept on straw and were not given uniforms for three months. At least the volunteers were fed well; one source claims that agricultural labourers who joined up put on a stone in weight in a month.[11]

The training that faced these volunteers was a nineteenth-century traditional system designed to make soldiers out of petty criminals and wastrels. They were subjected to fierce discipline and severe punishments, designed to make them obey without question. Most New-Army battalions were trained by a few retired officers and old N.C.O.s, whose tactical ideas were already out of date. They concentrated on drill, which they knew well, and ignored the small scale actions which were to dominate the fighting. The British Army had learned some lessons from the Boer War, but they largely ignored the tactical development brought about by the machine gun. Partly due to shortage of ammunition, rifle shooting was neglected. During a six month period of training with the 3rd Norfolks, Harry Smith only had four shooting sessions.

At the beginning of the war very few officers were promoted from the ranks. The Kitchener battalions often selected or even elected their N.C.O.s from the ranks, mostly men with some professional or managerial experience. The N.C.O.s appointed by the 8th Norfolks in October 1914 included a large contingent of journalists from the *Eastern Daily Press*. The military authorities trusted background rather than experience in the newly commissioned officers that they drafted into the new battalions. The 2/6th Norfolk cyclists received as subalterns boys who had been cadet sergeants with Stonyhurst College, and Repton Officer Training Corps, and ex-privates from the elite London territorial battalion, the Artists Rifles. Cambridgeshire battalions drew their officers largely from the Cambridge University O.T.C. The training given to officers was inadequate for the demands of trench warfare. As late as the spring of 1916 the Infantry Officers' basic course of one month at the School of Musketry was devoting a complete week to firing the rifle in the standing position, and only two hours to platoon tactics.

In preserving the class structure of British society in its military structure, the rank and file were given little opportunity for individual initiative. In the words of the *Official History*: 'When British troops lost their officers they were . . . apt to fall back, not because they were beaten, but because they did not know what to do and expected fresh orders.'

The New Army had very high morale, but its training was an insult to the high calibre of recruits in its ranks. As a result, when faced with the realities of trench warfare, New Army battalions were found to be badly trained and less adaptable when compared with Australian, German or French formations.

There was widespread distrust of the New Army by many British generals. When it was first tested on a large scale on the first day of the Somme, pages of precise instructions were issued even down to platoon level. However, this attention to detail could not make good deficiencies in basic training, and when strict timetables and artillery barrages broke down when faced with German resistance, it actually caused more confusion and bloodshed. The enormous local pride of the East Anglian battalions was no match for uncut wire and German machine guns.

The military authorities were not only wasteful of men's lives, but also of the skills which were necessary in a modern army. Arthur Johnson of West Winch, a skilled fitter at Savages of King's Lynn, served two years with the Norfolk Territorials before being transferred to work on aircraft for the Royal Naval Air Service, and later in the R.A.F. (Incidentally, this made him one of the few men to have served in the Army, Navy and Air Force.) Bill Curtis of Salhouse, a steam traction engine operator, was wounded and gassed serving in a Norfolk Kitchener battalion before his skills were recognised as useful to the Railway Operating Department.

Conscription
The war resulted in huge casualties to the British Army which needed replacing. Once the men likely to volunteer in each rural community had gone, fewer people came forward. The bombardment of East Coast ports by the German Navy stimulated recruitment for a time at the end of 1914, but it had soon reduced to a trickle. The *Eastern Weekly Press* reported on 7 November, that 'only 50% of those eligible in Norfolk have come forward'. The Liberal government moved slowly towards conscription, perhaps aware that by disregarding one of its basic principles of individual freedom, it was thereby signing its own death warrant. The National Registration Act was followed by Lord Derby's Scheme where men would 'attest' that they were ready to serve if called on, and where single men would be taken before married men. These failed to produce enough new soldiers, so in January 1916, conscription was introduced for single men, and extended to cover married men in June 1916.

There are explanations as to why voluntary recruiting dried up. The government, in its propaganda, stressed the positive side and continually said that Britain was winning. If this was so, many rural men saw no need to go. Walter Rye, a Norfolk journalist, started a lively correspondence in the *Eastern Daily Press* in August 1917 when he accused the farming community of being backward in enlisting. Using statistics from North and East Norfolk, he claimed only 15% of farmers and farmers' sons had enlisted compared with 42% of lawyers and 33% of clergy. Rye blamed the 'slower minds and greater personal interests (which) led them to stay at home and manage what has proved to be a most remunerative business'.

The news of conditions at the front were already circulating at home. The 7th Norfolks had arrived in France as early as May 1915, the 9th lost half its strength during its first action in September 1915, a mere eight days after landing in France. The losses of the territorials in Gallipoli, particularly the 'disappearance' of the Sandringham Company of the 1/5th Norfolks, were already known in the county. As the young and single with no ties had gone, those left behind with family responsibilities saw little reason to follow them. Edgar Wicks of East Rudham remembers his father coming back from the Attestation Board in Norwich: 'He was laughing and joking, but those that passed weren't laughing.'[12] In reporting a military tribunal case in March 1916, the *Eastern Weekly Press* could not help adding, but not naming the appellant as from 'one of the worst villages for recruiting'.

Casualties and Experiences

Kitchener's Army took part in its first major battle on the Somme on 1 July 1916. It suffered 60,000 casualties, mostly within the first two hours of the attack. Three service battalions of the Norfolk Regiment went 'over the top' on the first day of the Somme. The 7th lost 489 men, the 9th, 448, and the 8th, 105. (The 8th lost a further 662 men in the course of the next week's fighting.) All three battalions, consisting entirely of 1914 volunteers, ceased to exist as effective formations. Bill Curtis of Salhouse: 'Up on the Somme we went in a full battalion, we come out twenty-four of us. That's all what was left of us. The scouts what they had said the wire was all cut so we could get through, but when we got there that was all as good as ever and they mowed them down like sheep in front of the wire. When we couldn't get through we got in a shell hole. There was five people all from Salhouse in that shell. I was the only one that got back.'[13]

The local press in the summer of 1916 reported on a different world, with British advances on the Western Front. The heavy censorship precluded mention of local casualties, in contrast to the accurate and immediate reporting up until July 1916. Not until the end of August were the casualties of 1 July mentioned and this continued until the end of October alongside their photographs, with phrases like 'the following are reported on various dates'. There is no doubt that the authorities, by keeping information to a trickle, hoped to spread out the impact of 1 July. The only parallel with the losses of the urban 'Pals' battalions, where whole streets went into mourning, was the 11th Suffolks, the Cambridge battalion, which lost 527 men. Three of the author's great uncles were among the casualties of this battalion that morning.

The Norfolk battalions drew their men from all over the county, but even here the news of the slaughter on 1 July got through. Those men like Bill Curtis who did get back, described the reality of the fighting to families who had lost members. The 7th, 8th and 9th Norfolks were pulled out of the line, filled up with drafts and retrained. The 9th attacked again in October 1916, this time with tanks, but still lost 239 men. The authorities found it difficult to find enough Norfolk men, so drafted in others from all over the

27

country. Men were moved freely between battalions, and the War Office broke its pledge of 1914, not to move volunteers and territorials from their chosen units.

Opposition to the War
By the time conscription was introduced, war fever had subsided, and opposition to the war had taken shape. It was even evident among enlisted men. Most soldiers once in the grip of the military machine kept serving, either through natural conservatism or loyalty to groups of friends. The Commanding Officer of the 1st Cambridgeshires wrote in August 1916 that the average soldier went on 'because he did not like to let his pals down'.[14] The mutinies that occurred in the French and Russian armies in the field did not take place among the British. Nevertheless, there was a groundswell of passive resistance to military authority, the evidence of which is hazy and has now largely disappeared. Stories do come down of old scores settled in the heat of battle and of unpopular officers and tyrannical N.C.O.s being shot from behind. Some men simply gave up the will to live. My great uncle having been wounded on 1 July, was sent, on recovery, to a Scottish Highland unit. He was later gassed and returned to convalesce at his home in Cambridge, where he took his own life rather than face the prospect of another spell at the front. As late as January 1916, the *Eastern Weekly Press* published a report of Christmas fraternisation in the trenches in a letter from a private in the 1st Norfolks.

In adopting conscription, the Liberal government was abandoning one of the tenets of its faith. Many Liberal politicians, whilst not criticising the war effort, opposed conscription and helped conscientious objectors at tribunals. From 1916 onwards, the local press was full of tribunal hearings of individuals not wanting to be called up. Some of the individuals were Socialists, largely centred on the Independent Labour Party in Norwich, who saw the war as a diversion from class conflict. Others objected on religious grounds. Christadelphians and the Plymouth Brethren would have nothing to do with war or government, but the large Quaker community usually felt able to serve in the medical corps. The largest number of tribunal cases were from small businessmen and agricultural small-holders trying to get classified as reserved occupations to avoid closing down. From this generally apolitical group, one glimpses a profound sense of war weariness. Although the labour movement gradually became represented on the tribunals, their general tone was a jingoistic and bullying one.

At another level, many conscripts tried to fail their medicals. It is difficult to find evidence about how common this was, but stories do survive in family folklore. The author's uncle, conscripted in 1918, certainly tried eating soap to bring on palpitations of the heart, in an unsuccessful attempt to avoid service, after a premonition (unfortunately to become true) that he would not be returning from France.

Conscript Army

By 1917 the volunteer character of the army had changed. Ernie Cornwall of Syderstone recalled: 'When I went in in 1917 there weren't many volunteers. There might have been a few, but not many, you were called up!'[15] In Norfolk the recruiting sub-stations were gradually closed down. The Ministry of National Service took over military conscription and the posting of workers into vital industries through an army of civilian female clerks based in Norwich. They were backed by the military tribunals. The days of the recruiting sergeant at Hempton Fair were gone forever.

The increasing mechanisation of the war demanded specialised skills in units like the Engineers, Tanks, Machine Gun Corps, Flying Corps and Motor transport. Centralised authorities were much better placed to assess the skills of conscripted men, so much better use was made of manpower than in the early days of the war. Most of the older men, in particular, that were called up, were slotted into support units, while the young Norfolk agricultural labourers went into the infantry. None of the men I interviewed who were called up, were in the Norfolk Regiment. They served in a variety of units ranging from the West Surreys to the West Yorkshires. They were transferred between units frequently as the contingencies of the war demanded, and no attempt was made to establish a local link with the unit. This did have the advantage that localities were not unduly affected when the units which bore their names were decimated on the battlefield. There was to be no repeat of the first day of the Somme.

It became increasingly difficult for county regiments, like the Norfolks, to keep up the strength of their Service Battalions. The new fruitful recruiting grounds were in the cities. Consequently, during the army reorganisation of January 1918, the 8th Norfolk Regiment was disbanded and the men moved to the 7th and 9th Battalions. In the Suffolk Regiment, both the 8th and 9th battalions were disbanded. In the Middle East, the first and second line territorial battalions of the Norfolks were amalgamated after heavy casualties in the battles around Gaza.

The local character and pride of 1914 was replaced by 1918, by a younger, more homogenous and in some ways, a more skilled army. Some authorities claim that the British army collapsed in March 1918 under the German offensive, and many conscript units filled with raw recruits did surrender en masse. A photograph survives in the collection at the Norfolk Rural Life Museum showing five young conscripts all with different caps or cap badges, taken in January 1918. Three of the five were captured in March 1918, and all safely returned from the war. Part of a draft to the 1st Cambridgeshires was thus described: 'The other 300 were boys called up in the Spring. Their average length of service was about fifteen weeks. They had fired a musketry course but knew nothing about Lewis guns. They had come straight from the base and had never been under fire.'[16] However, it was the same young conscripts who learned to become proficient in the horrific techniques of trench warfare. In doing so the training methods current at the beginning of the war had become adapted to encourage individual initiative on the part of each soldier. The tactical unit was now the platoon or even the section rather than the battalion. Now led by officers of whom two-thirds were promoted from the ranks, this young army drove the Germans back from August 1918 until the end of the war. The imposition of a rigid class structure by the military authorities, particularly in their comparative reluctance to accept as officers rankers who were good at their jobs, instead of boys from the 'right' social background, was responsible for needless loss of life in the first three years of the war.

The Cost
Censorship could not conceal the extent of the huge casualties that continued to be suffered, but somehow East Anglia had adjusted to these losses. Proportionally, Norfolk suffered about an average war loss. One hundred thousand men had served, out of a population of half a million. Twelve thousand of these had died, and tens of thousands were wounded. Six thousand had been killed in the ranks of the Norfolk Regiment, a third of these in the Battle of the Somme.[17]

Some men could not settle in civilian lives after such horrendous experiences, and re-joined the army. Some sought out the company of men who had shared that life in the British Legion, which had absorbed the more radical ex-service organisations in 1920. Some simply disappeared. Private Ted Hunt of Attleborough joined the Suffolks in 1914 and was never heard of again by his relatives. Half of the war dead had no known graves. All families found it difficult to live with these disappearances, and many cherished hopes that their loved ones were still alive. But as the prisoners of war returned, these hopes became desperate. A poignant advertisement appeared in *The Times* of 4 January 1919 from Guy Davey of Aldborough near Norwich requesting that 'Any information concerning Major S. Davey, 40th Bn. Machine Gun Corps, who was reported missing at Ervillers on 25th March 1918 will be gratefully received'.[18]

Some men simply returned and took up civilian life where they left off, seemingly completely unaffected by their experiences. Farmworkers were among the first to be released from the forces at the end of the war. This may explain why East Anglian units were generally exempt from the confused and generally unrecorded protests of the bored and sullen soldiers awaiting demobilisation. Towns and parishes sometimes organised tea parties for returning soldiers, often delaying them until well into 1919;

'Peace Day' in July was a suitable date. But these were sad, ill-attended affairs, however well meant, and little prepared the returning soldier for what he would meet in civilian life.

Some never adjusted to peace time society, and regarded the time when they had joined together in an unprecedented display of local and national pride as the highlight of their lives. The war followed most veterans to their graves. As the author's great uncle was dying in 1968, he was, in his delirium, back in the trenches of fifty years before, a sergeant in the Suffolks, issuing orders to repel a German raid.

Notes

1. Sir Henry Rider Haggard, *A Farmer's Year*, London, 1899, pp. 75–6.
2. E. Riddell and M. C. Clayton, *The Cambridgeshires 1914 to 1919*, Cambridge, 1934, p. 1.
3. Interviewed by Alun Howkins and quoted in his book *Poor Labouring Men*, London, 1985, p. 116.
4. Reported in *Norfolk News*, 19 September 1914.
5. Ibid.
6. Interview by author 1983. Tape at Norfolk Rural Life Museum, Gressenhall.
7. *Norfolk News*, 12 September 1914.
8. Interview by author 1983. Tape at Norfolk Rural Life Museum, Gressenhall.
9. Interview and transcript Imperial War Museum Sound Records Department.
10. *Norfolk News*, 26 September 1914.
11. Denis Winter, *Death's Men: Soldiers of the Great War*, London, 1978, p. 231.
12. Interview by author, 1982.
13. Interview by author, 1983. Tape at Norfolk Rural Life Museum, Gressenhall.
14. Riddell and Clayton, op. cit., p. 41.
15. Interview by author, 1983. Tape at Norfolk Rural Life Museum, Gressenhall.
16. Riddell and Clayton, op. cit., p. 216.
17. Martin Bates, *East Anglia: The Regional Military Histories*, London, 1974, and Programme of Memorial Service at Norwich Cathedral, 4 September 1919.
18. *The Times*, 4 January 1919. Quoted in Winter, op., cit., p. 256.

The New Technology:
Threat from Air and Sea

by
Nicholas Forder

In Britain fear of the products of the so-called 'new technology' was already well established prior to the outbreak of war. Noted technical advances in aerial and nautical navigation, together with the contemporary theory of endless progress, provided the fuel for imaginations contemplating a dreadful new kind of warfare. It was not an image of warfare stagnated by artillery, machine guns and entrenchments; a warfare based on attrition; that took root in the fertile minds of the British public. Concepts were more grandiose, more akin to the flights of fancy of Jules Verne and H. G. Wells; the public foresaw war expanded into the third dimension: under the seas and above the waves. It must be remembered that in 1914 Britain's position as a world power was secured by the dominance of the Royal Navy. In 1914 there seemed reason enough to believe that this dominance could be overcome by stealth. That 'damned un-English weapon', the submarine, had demonstrated great promise; but it was Bleriot's cross-channel flight of 1909 that convinced large sections of the British public of Lord Northcliffe's assertion that 'Britain is no longer an island'. When war broke out the prospect of serious disruption of overseas trade and bombardment, perhaps even invasion, from the air seemed real enough.

However, war first came to East Anglia in a more conventional form on 3 November 1914 when Great Yarmouth was bombarded by the German High Seas Fleet. Fortunately, due to a miscalculation – the German ships were over the horizon and thus unable to see where their shells were actually landing – the town suffered damage no greater than the rearrangement of the sand on its famous beaches. Of course the damage done to the town's dignity was incalculable, especially when the Royal Navy failed to appear immediately and put the raiders to flight. In fact the Navy was engaged in the form of two gunboats, one of which was Yarmouth's own H.M.S. *Halcyon*, and two accompanying destroyers. Clearly these were no match for the German battlecruisers, and the former's actions were more in the nature of a fighting withdrawal. Submarines from the naval base situated on the Gorleston side of the Haven also tried to intervene as the

33

Germans departed. As the Germans did so they laid a screen of mines, one of which claimed the pursuing submarine D5.

The possibility of such a raid had been forseen since the 1860s, the only difference being that then the enemy was perceived as being France. The truth was that such was the extent of Britain's coastline and the speed of the German warships that it was physically impossible to prevent such raids, and the region continued to suffer from sporadic enemy naval action throughout the war. Of these subsequent raids the most significant was carried out on Lowestoft some eighteen months later on 25 April 1916. One of the witnesses of this raid, and others, was Dame Margery Corbett-Ashby: 'We were roused by the well known window shaking and watched the searchlights beyond Yarmouth. At 4.15 or 20 there was a terrific noise. I was by Michael's (her son) side in a moment, you could hardly hear anyone speak for the noise . . . The damage is amazingly small considering that an unexploded shell by the sands is 12½ inches in diameter and is larger than Brian's (her husband's) walking stick . . . The houses round are punctured by fragments mostly over 15 lbs in weight. We only had a small piece in the roof and another through the greenhouse. We don't yet know the casualties, a big double fronted house was struck by a direct hit and sliced nearly in half and caught fire, one man was killed instantly. There were a good many casualties by the pier I fancy.'[1] The latter is almost certainly a reference to the sightseers watching the German gun flashes.

Though essentially only nuisance raids, or attempts to bring sections of the Royal Navy's Grand Fleet to action, these bombardments by the German Navy were frequent enough to encourage evacuation of coastal areas as Dame Margery noted: 'The Hall family left this morning, also Mrs Fritton and the Child family. The Dixons go tomorrow so Michael will be the only babe but one left!' Dame Margery also indicated the importance that the British government placed on suppressing news and specific details of the damage caused by enemy action: 'I mustn't tell you the various stories in a letter as it will never reach you.' This was done not so much as to reduce fears of widespread panic, but so as to deny the German intelligence. This policy was officially inaugurated on 5 May 1915 when the Government issued Defence Notice D206 requesting editors not to publish material disclosing useful information. After the war one Zeppelin commander, Baron von Buttlar Brandenfels, freely admitted that he had altered one of his raid reports after reading an article in a neutral Dutch newspaper!

A prime example of 'German frightfulness' the sea bombardments of the East Coast certainly were, but they paled into insignificance compared to the Zeppelin threat; though the threat was to prove rather empty. In 1914

[1] Corbett-Ashby papers from part of Peter Liddle's 1914–18 Personal Experience Archive.

the Germans had yet to conceive a strategy for the use of their airships. The German people expected the Zeppelins to be used as bombers, and bombing trials had indeed been undertaken, but no stocks existed and the first 'bombs' dropped in anger by a Zeppelin were actually crudely modified naval shells. Despite contemporary popular belief, few of the high ranking officers of either the German Army or Navy believed that the Zeppelin was a war winner in its own right. Admiral von Tirpitz openly opposed the idea of using Zeppelins as bombers believing, rightly, that they would be better employed as scouts for naval surface vessels. There was a plan for the bombing of mainland Britain in 1914, but this was expected to be carried out by aeroplanes. In the event no bases near enough to the coast were secured to overcome the range limitations of the early German bombers and the plan was postponed. Use of the Zeppelins was the only alternative. Nevertheless there still remained one obstacle and, ironically perhaps, that was the Kaiser himself. Despite the picture conjured up by British wartime propaganda, the Kaiser was genuinely concerned that Britain's historical monuments might be destroyed by bombing and, worse, that a member of the British Royal Family might be injured. It must be remembered that in 1914 the British, German and Russian royal families were all related, leading to one description of the Great War as being merely a 'family squabble'. A number of factors combined to change the Kaiser's mind, including German public opinion, civilian fatalities as a result of a French air raid on Karlsruhe, and Royal Naval Air Service raids on the Zeppelin bases at Düsseldorf and Friedrichshafen.

On 19 January 1915 the first Zeppelin raid was launched against Britain. The attacking force consisted of the naval airships L.3, L.4 and L.6. The designated targets were the Humber for the former two airships, and the Thames for the latter. None of these targets were actually reached. L.6 was forced to turn back with engine trouble, and L.3 and L.4 bombed what would now be termed as 'targets of opportunity'. Thus it was that Great Yarmouth suffered the first airship raid of the war. Kapitainleutnant Fritz, commander of L.3, on discovering that he had crossed the coast further south than intended, decided to drop his bombs on the clearly lit Yarmouth. Despite government calls for a 'black-out', in 1915, even off-season, few holiday resorts were prepared to risk losing trade by turning off their 'illuminations'. Fritz had merely to take a bearing from the Winterton and Happisburgh light ships and follow the coast line towards the bright lights. Throughout the war the Happisburgh lightship was to prove an invaluable navigation aid for the attacking Zeppelins. The lightship was never moved because it was too important as a navigation aid to British coastal trade, and it also made the approach route of the raiding airships more predictable. Later in the war the aircraft from the Great Yarmouth Air Station were dispersed to a number of small landing grounds thus allowing them to patrol across these predicted flight paths. Misleading lights were also shown, in the age old tradition of the East Coast wreckers.

The Germans considered Great Yarmouth to be a legitimate target by virtue of the submarine and air bases situated there. Thus Fritz ordered the first bomb to be dropped as L.3 passed over Norfolk Square, and continued bombing as the airship followed an approximate north to south route over the town. The actual number of bombs dropped will probably never be known; many were dropped in pairs, at least one fell in the Haven, and even the contemporary newspapers disagreed. None of the town's military targets were damaged, but a 53 year old cobbler, Samuel Smith, and a 72 year old spinster, Martha Taylor, made history by becoming the first fatal casualties of an air raid on Great Britain. At the victims' inquest the Coroner said 'that the unfortunate man and woman were victims of so-called warfare – but he did not call it so. It was the offspring of German culture. It was contrary to International Law to attack any unfortified place, such as Yarmouth was. But the Germans were past masters in regarding anything in the form of writing as a mere "scrap of paper"' (*G.Y. Independent*, 23.1.1915). The 'scrap of paper' was the term used by Germany to dismiss her undertaking to recognise Belgium's neutrality, the violation of which had caused Britain's entry into the Great War. The newspapers were also full of eyewitness accounts of the raid, many of which were confused and contradictory. Horace Potts, local doctor and reputed M.I.5 man, recounted his version of the raid to a reporter from the *Great Yarmouth Independent*:

'One of the local doctors, who hurriedly organised a search of the town to deal with any cases which might need urgent attention, gave a vivid account of the raid. "It was my maid who was the first of our household to notice the Zeppelin," he said. "She was attracted to it by a brilliant searchlight, which shone down straight from the sky upon the house. (This was more likely a parachute flare.) It was between 8.30 and 9.00. She ran out into the garden and there she could hear the hum of the engines, and almost immediately there was a violent explosion on St Peter's Plain at the back of the street in which I lived." He promptly made his way to the scene. "It was pitch dark," he continued, "and the streets were littered with broken glass and the ruins of doors and window frames. There was no panic, however, just a little natural excitement. In St Peter's Plain two houses on opposite sides of the way had been demolished, and I understand that neither of them was occupied. I found in a passage a man (Samuel Smith) with his head blown off, and I was picking my way along when I stumbled over another prostrate body. Quickly I struck a match and it proved to be that of an elderly woman whose side had been partially blown away. She was quite dead. (Martha

Taylor.) Both of these persons had been killed by the explosion on the Plain, and they lay from 20 to 30 yards from the ruins. I was told that several injured persons had been removed to hospital. Personally, I did not see the airships; but I was informed that there had been two over the town, and that altogether they dropped at least five bombs. (There was only one airship, and it dropped approximately twelve bombs.)'

The *Yarmouth Mercury*, for 23 January, contained an interview with one of the residents of St Peter's Plain:

'Next door, No. 18, Mrs Scott had a wonderful escape. Her husband, who has joined the A.S.C. (Army Service Corps), left her on Monday for Woolwich, so that she was all alone with her little child of two when this dreadful explosion occurred. Immediately she was in total darkness, and all around her were falling things. She had heard the whirr of a propeller, and had she not been dressing her baby she would have gone to the front door – in all probability to a horrible death. "I think my child saved my life. Then when the gas went out I dropped the babe on the floor in order to get a light again. I had to leave it screaming while I did so." The light revealed the utter ruin of her home. The front door had been torn off and flung across the room, only just missing her as she sat near the table. Windows, blinds, curtains, pictures, chairs – everything was smashed. Marvellous to say, the baby was not scratched, and though Mrs Scott's face was streaming in blood, it was found to be nothing worse than a number of cuts from flying bits of glass. "I feel I cannot be thankful enough to think I am not smashed to pieces."'

L.4, meanwhile, had flown around the north Norfolk coast dropping bombs on various targets including Sheringham, Hunstanton, Grimston (near Sandringham) and King's Lynn. Two more civilians were killed in Lynn, a woman and a young boy. In addition to the fatalities the two Zeppelins had injured a further sixteen civilians and caused damage estimated at £7,740. One result of the raid was that many people purchased 'Aircraft and Bombardment Insurance' policies, a number of which had been available since 1914 including a Government scheme. The raid also marked a change in attitude; more than the seaborne bombardments it signified to ordinary civilians that the Great War was their war, and many were eager to participate in it. Of course the outrage caused by the 'Hun baby-killers' was used as an aid to recruiting, but many people chose to search out the enemy in their midst. After the raid a number of reports were made of lights and 'spies' in motor cars directing the Zeppelins to their targets. No one asked that if this was so then why hadn't the raid been more effective? Clearly it was not a matter for rational reflection. The use of a motor car's headlights as a navigation aid had been pioneered by Claude

Grahame-White during his 1910 London to Manchester flight, and this widely reported event caught the public imagination. The M.P. for King's Lynn, Holcombe Ingleby, after asking questions in the House of Commons, even felt sufficiently motivated to write a book, *The Zeppelin Raid in West Norfolk*, to draw people's attention to the presence of 'German spies'. The subject of German spies was not always taken seriously, though. Just as the *Yarmouth Mercury* had produced a cartoon suggesting possible comical consequences of the blackout, it also printed a report on the activities of an overzealous would-be spycatcher: Following a report from a citizen that he was sure that his neighbour was regularly signalling information to U-boats and Zeppelins, as the former heard constant and unexplained tapping noises, like a morse-key, coming from his neighbour's back yard, the police decided to investigate. Fortunately, for the state of security of the nation, the unexplained 'tapping' was revealed to be nothing more sinister than a dog chained to a wooden kennel!

There was also concern over more practical matters, chief among which was the failure of the aeroplanes from the air stations to intercept and destroy the raiders. The truth of the matter was that R.N.A.S. Great Yarmouth had not been officially informed of the presence of the Zeppelins until after L.3 had dropped the last of its load and was heading back out over the North Sea. With no definite information as to the whereabouts of the airships it appeared futile, and even dangerous, for aircraft to attempt to pursue in the dark. Even if the naval aeroplanes had been able to locate the airships, then the latter's superior performance would have allowed them to simply outclimb and evade their pursuers. Anti-Zeppelin weapons were also sadly lacking in early 1915. The Royal Naval Air Service had been experimenting with various weapons, including the ingenious fiery grapnel which was intended to be towed by the attacking aeroplane in the hope that the grapnel might be attached to the airship's fabric. Of the 200 Hales anti-Zeppelins grenades produced prior to the outbreak of war, twenty-two had been used for experimental work and none of the others were stored at Great Yarmouth. The nearest supply was at Felixstowe, and the Royal Naval Air Station there only possessed twelve. *The War in the Air*, the official history, notes that pilots were supposed to ram enemy airships if no other means to destroy them was available. Fortunately such drastic measures were never called for. But it was not until June 1916 that incendiary ammunition became available, and then initially only in small quantities. Nevertheless, progress was made, mainly in the sphere of organisation of defences, and by the end of 1916 no less than six German airships had been destroyed. One of these was L.21, brought down in the early hours of 28 November by three pilots from R.N.A.S. Great Yarmouth.

On 28 November 1916 L.21 was one of a ten airship force which set out to bomb targets in the Midlands and on Tyneside. After the rather ineffectual bombing of towns in the Potteries, L.21 followed a somewhat laborious route back towards the Wash. Why this was so is not clear, though it seems likely that the commander of L.21, Kapitainleutnant Frankenberg, was unsure of his navigation, or possibly the airship was suffering with engine problems. En route to the Wash, L.21 was spotted by no less than three defending aeroplanes, all of which failed to intercept, before reaching the coast at Great Yarmouth. By now the defences had been fully alerted, and gunfire from the harbour defences directed three naval B.E. 2c aircraft towards the Zeppelin. These aircraft were flown by Flight Lieutenant Egbert Cadbury, Flight Sub-Lieutenant G. W. R. Fane, and Flight Sub-Lieutenant E. L. Pulling. The former two had taken off from the naval landing ground at Burgh Castle, and the latter from Bacton. Cadbury was the first to spot L.21 and began his attack from 700 feet below the airship, firing four drums of ammunition from his single Lewis gun as he closed. Meanwhile, Fane had closed to within 100 feet of the airship's starboard side only to find that his Lewis gun had jammed due to frozen lubricating oil. Frustrated, Fane attempted to climb above the Zeppelin in order to attempt a bombing attack. Though this might seem a rather bizarre tactic, it had been successfully employed by Flight Sub-Lieutenant R. A. J. Warneford on 7 June 1915 when he attacked Zeppelin LZ 37, and thus became the first airman to destroy a Zeppelin in flight. It was now Pulling's turn to attack, and he opened fire from about fifty feet below the airship, but his gun jammed after only a few rounds. Pulling turned away to clear the jam, and, as he did so, he saw L.21 ignite towards its stern. Within seconds the Zeppelin was a blazing hulk, and the fragile giant fell into the sea off Lowestoft some nine minutes after Cadbury had first spotted it. There were no survivors.

The events of the latter part of 1916 virtually put to rest the spectre of the Zeppelin. Though the Germans refined existing technology to make their airships more elusive they could not overcome the innate flaw of the design: the dependence on the potentially highly inflammable hydrogen as a lifting gas. The aeroplane soon proved to have greater potential for technological advance as a weapon of war. Performance, however, did not play a direct and very significant role in gaining air supremacy over the British Isles. The mainstay of the British air defence in 1918 was still a variant of the B.E.2, a pre-war design which had fulfilled the role of nightfighter throughout the war. It was the better organisation of the defences which produced results. An illustration of this is that although the 'R' type Zeppelin, introduced into service in May 1916, was capable of operating at a height at which it would take the standard British nightfighter fifty or sixty minutes to reach, this was irrelevant if the defenders had sufficient advance warning to establish patrols at the right height and in the right area.

Significant influence of the improvement in aeroplane performance was exerted on the airship force from an unexpected quarter. On 25 May 1917, twenty-one German Gothas bombed Folkestone in daylight. The results of the raid were 95 killed, a further 195 injured, and damage estimated at £19,405. A total of seventy-seven defence sorties were flown against the raiders; all were unsuccessful. One Gotha was lost, but this fell victim to aircraft from R.N.A.S. Dunkirk, on the return flight. It seemed that the Gotha would easily supplant the airship as a strategic bomber, and if it had not been for the devoted efforts of a few, such as Fregattenkapitain Peter Strasser, this would certainly have been accepted earlier. Unfortunately for Strasser his convictions were to be proved wrong in the worst possible way: he was a passenger in L.70, destroyed by a D.H. 4 nightfighter from R.N.A.S. Great Yarmouth on 5 August 1918.

Although, as previously mentioned, the B.E. 2 emerged as the most successful Zeppelin fighter of the war there were many other new designs built specially to counter the threat. The majority of these proved of limited usefulness, but all were thoroughly tested. Most of this testing, together with research and development work, was carried out in Suffolk. New aircraft types were tested at Martlesham Heath, and from 1915 the Royal Flying Corps' Experimental Flying Section was stationed at Orfordness. The work undertaken at the latter covered all spheres of aerial warfare from bombing to early radar. In late 1916 34 (Reserve) Squadron was also based there, and on 4 October Captain Albert Ball, D.S.O., M.C., joined this unit. Ball was then the top scoring British scout pilot and his posting was the result of anxiety generated by the inadequate system of training student pilots, many of whom seemed to last only a matter of days after being posted to one of the squadrons fighting on the Western Front. However, the transfer of experienced pilots to training squadrons was an insufficient remedy. Instructing remains very much a specialist task, and exceptionally good pilots seldom make good instructors. Allied to this is the often repeated claim that successful scout pilots were foremost good shots, and sometimes indifferent pilots. For a loner like Ball the task must have seemed impossible, especially as the tactics he employed were little more complex than attacking enemy formations whenever he encountered them and trusting in the element of surprise. Ball's time at Orfordness must have been rather unhappy as he spent a great deal of his time attempting to gain either a transfer back to France or to be allowed to help fight the Zeppelins. Permission for the latter was constantly refused, though this was not always so as two aircraft from the Experimental Station participated in the destruction of L.48 on the night of 16/17 June 1917. Ball had to wait until April 1917 before he was in action again. A month later he was dead. Though a far from ideal instructor, Ball was a great inspiration to the R.F.C. pilots who followed him and to many Ball became the epitome of the young Englishman 'doing his duty for King and Country'.

There were many other training stations in Norfolk and Suffolk, and by 1918 they had become too numerous to mention. This was a phenomenon unique to the Great War, for by the outbreak of the Second World War the increased range of military aircraft forced the training stations to be situated further from the coast of mainland Europe. It should also be said that not everyone found instructing in East Anglia quite as frustrating as Albert Ball. James McCudden, V.C., D.S.O., M.M., recalled a very pleasant day shooting hare and partridge, with a service rifle, while stationed at Sedgeford in Norfolk. His enjoyment was only slightly marred when the station commanding officer informed him that he had not only been shooting game out of season, he had also been poaching. Why McCudden's actions were so frowned upon seems strange in light of the knowledge that the officers of one of Sedgeford's resident units, 64 Squadron, used to regularly go wild fowling with Lewis machine guns in order to improve their marksmanship.

Not all R.F.C. training was carried out in mainland Britain, and one of those taught to fly in the Middle East was Henry Montgomery Scott Pillow of Castle Meadow, Norwich. A dental student at Guy's Hospital on the outbreak of war, Harry Scott Pillow was just one of the many young men who 'postponed' their careers in order to 'do their bit'. Pillow joined the 18th Battalion of the Royal Fusiliers, before being commissioned in the Middlesex Regiment and being attached to the Royal Flying Corps for pilot training. After gaining his 'ticket' with the 20th (Reserve) Wing at Aboukir, Pillow returned to 20th (Training) Squadron at Wyton. There he undertook his advanced training before being posted to 7 Squadron on 30 July 1917. 7 Squadron, based at Droglandt west of Ypres, was then engaged in artillery observation and photo reconnaissance duties. The Squadron had been re-equipping with R.E. 8 aircraft since June, but as Pillow was a new pilot he would almost certainly have been allocated one of the Squadron's older B.E. 2e aircraft. The B.E. 2 had been conceived as a stable platform for reconnaissance, a virtue which made it a very good nightfighter, but such aircraft were obsolete by July 1917. Slow, unmanouverable, inadequately armed and with the observer/gunner in a position which seriously limited his field of fire, the B.E. 2e was still expected to defend itself against the latest Albatros and Halberstadt scouts. The impact of technical developments is perhaps best illustrated by the air war over the Western Front where the introduction of a new type of scout could briefly claim local air superiority and find the vulnerable two-seaters unprotected. Harry Scott Pillow joined 7 Squadron at a time when the R.F.C. were recovering from the mauling known as 'Bloody April' and the Albatros scout still reigned supreme. On 13 October 1917, H. Sankey of 7 Squadron recorded: 'I heard

41

from men of the battery Scott Pillow was working with that he was brought down by a German machine. Lt. Pillow was attacked by three German machines. He did for two of them (i.e. he evaded their attacks), but the third got him from the back. He fell behind our lines and was taken to a farmhouse and one of our doctors attended to him but he died half an hour afterwards. He was brought down and buried at Proven just behind Poperinge.

He'd only been with us for three weeks or a month. He was a splendid officer.'

It was actually Harry Scott Pillow's ninth day with the Squadron.

It would be naive to attribute Harry Scott Pillow's death solely to his obsolete aircraft, but it is difficult not to regard it as a contributing factor. This was not really the fault of R.F.C. Headquarters; the root of the problem probably lay with pre-war political decisions which led to the R.F.C.'s virtual dependence on the products of the Royal Aircraft Factory designers and the consequential lack of encouragement given to smaller private manufacturers. When the war created an increased demand for both aero engines and airframes the smaller manufacturers took time to expand, and a partial solution to the immediate problem was standardisation. This policy was also to be pursued, in the face of some criticism, during the Second World War. Though it resulted in the production of a large number of aircraft it often resulted in aircraft types being manufactured after the design had become obsolete. In an attempt to increase the manufacturing capabilities of the British aircraft industry a number of companies who had no previous experience of aircraft manufacture were granted contracts. These were mostly engineering firms or those with experience of working in wood. In Norfolk these companies included the Norwich based Boulton and Paul Ltd. and Mann Egerton and Co. Ltd., Frederick Sage and Co. of Peterborough and Savages Ltd. of King's Lynn. In Suffolk the firms of Richard Garrett and Sons of Leiston, and Ransomes, Sims and Jeffries of Ipswich also participated.

Re-organisation of these companies took time. Mann Egerton had to construct an erection shop on Aylsham Road in Norwich, and there was the problem of plans and blueprints from which to work. It is no exaggeration to say that aircraft design was still essentially at the stage when calculations were made on the backs of old envelopes, and the outline of a new aircraft design was chalked out on the workshop floor. In mid-1915 Mann Egerton received its first order when it was selected by the Admiralty to be one of six contractors to build the Short designed type 184 seaplane. As no working drawings were available, Shorts provided a sample aircraft for inspection by draughtsmen from each of the companies. Each draughtsman produced six sets of drawings of one particular part of the aircraft. By sending one of these copies to each contractor all received a full set of drawings. Until the end of the war it remained common practice for a sample aircraft to be supplied to contractors from which to work.

Before the end of the war some of these newly fledged aircraft manufacturers were producing their own designs. Boulton and Paul produced the Bobolink as an unsuccessful rival to the Sopwith Snipe as a Sopwith Camel replacement. Bearing in mind that Boulton and Paul built a large number of Camels, one of which still exists in the R.A.F. Museum, it is not surprising that the Bobolink displayed distinct signs of Sopwith influence. Likewise the Mann Egerton H1 and H2 shipboard fighter designs: these were unsuccessful rivals to the Sopwith 2F1 'ships' Camel, and featured some similarities with the French designed SPAD 7 scout of which Mann Egerton had built a number.

Of these Great War aircraft manufacturers, only Boulton and Paul continued to build aircraft after the Armistice. The Sidestrand and Overstrand bombers, the latter being the first aircraft to feature a power operated gun turret, were produced in Norfolk prior to the aircraft division of the company moving to the Midlands in the 1930s. Once there the company acquired a degree of notoriety by producing the Defiant which was, like the B.E. 2e, a refined interpretation of an obsolete concept.

Mention must also be made of the work of John Porte and the development of the Felixstowe flying boats at the naval air station of that name. Porte, invalided out of the Royal Naval Air Service, had been engaged by the American Curtiss Company to fly one of the latter's flying boats across the Atlantic in 1915. Obviously the outbreak of war made such a flight impossible. The flying boat designed specially for the flight, the Curtiss H-4 'America', was purchased by the Royal Navy together with a second boat. The 'America' was underpowered and suffered from very bad handling characteristics. However in 1915 it was the best available and the Navy ordered twelve more. The 'Americas' demonstrated the potential of the flying boat, but it was clear that an aircraft with better performance was necessary, and thus the Curtiss Company responded with the H-8 'Large America'. The Royal Navy ordered fifty of these flying boats which had both greater range and a greater load carrying capability. The first of the 'Large Americas' arrived at R.N.A.S. Felixstowe in July 1916. Early trials were disappointing with the 'Large America' proving to be underpowered like its predecessor. Porte, recalled to service and holding the rank of Wing Commander as station commander at Felixstowe, re-engined two of the 'Large Americas' with 250 h.p. Rolls Royce Eagles. This modification constituted a power increase of more than 50%. The design was accepted by the Royal Navy and ordered in quantity as the Curtiss H-12. Later modifications to the hull design of the Curtiss resulted in a series of flying boats designated 'F' and commonly referred to as the 'Felixstowe boats'.

Unfortunately the Curtiss H-12 flying boats were not operational until 13

April 1917, when the first example was delivered to R.N.A.S. Great Yarmouth. Until the arrival of these flying boats the Royal Naval Air Service was largely dependent on a variety of seaplane designs to undertake patrols over coastal shipping lanes and the North Sea searching for U-boats. With perhaps two exceptions, the Sopwith Baby and later versions of the Short 184, these seaplanes were of indifferent quality. They were fragile, and lack of research into float design meant that these aircraft were fitted with inadequate pontoons lacking a 'step' in their undersides. This meant that it was very difficult for the seaplane to break contact with the water in unfavourable conditions, and also that loads had to be kept to a minimum. As a result many of the so-called two-seaters were actually employed as single-seaters to enable them to carry something approaching a useful warload. There were also some particular problems concerning seaplane operations at Great Yarmouth: the aircraft had to operate from the open sea and thus suffered badly if the sea was rough. There was also the 144 feet high Nelson's Monument (The Norfolk Pillar) which represented a severe hazard to navigation, particularly at night. A far from ideal site for an air station, the South Denes had been chosen largely for reasons of economy. The land was made available to the Admiralty for a very low rental, and the nearby Coastguard Station was considered suitable to accommodate the initial establishment of two officers and five ratings.

Ill-equipped though the Royal Naval Air Service was, it still had to counter another threat even greater than the Zeppelin: the submarine. Like the airship the submarine was virtually untried as a weapon of war in 1914. Certainly there was reason to fear it because of its ability to operate invisible to the naked eye. However these early submarines were not 'submarines' in the true sense: they were submersibles. Certainly they were capable of travelling underwater but only for relatively short periods of time, and even then only at very slow speeds. Dependent on rechargeable batteries for undersea navigation, submarines mostly travelled on the surface and, contrary to popular belief, usually used their deck armament, rather than torpedoes, to sink their targets. Despite these limitations, during the two periods of unrestricted submarine warfare (application of the so-called 'sink on sight' policy contrary to International Law which stated that merchant-men must be boarded to ensure that they were carrying contraband of war) from May to September 1915 and from February 1917, U-boats were ensuring that up to 25% of British merchantmen failed to complete return voyages. The tide began to turn in May 1917 for the two common reasons: better equipment and improved organisation. The introduction into service of the Curtiss H-12 flying boats facilitated long duration standing patrols by wireless equipped well armed aircraft. These were utilised to fly in a new search pattern known as 'The Spider's Web'. Centred on the North Hinder lightship, which was situated in the main transit route for U-boats passing into the eastern end of the English Channel, the 'Web' was octagonal in shape and sixty miles in diameter. By following the 'lines' of the web aircraft could systematically search all or part of the 4,000 square miles enclosed by the octagonal. The advantage of the system soon became apparent as within the first two weeks of its introduction no fewer than eight U-boats were spotted by aircraft, three of which were attacked. The first successful attack probably occurred on 22 September 1917, though there were earlier unsubstantiated claims by flying boat crews.

It was, however, not essential that the U-boats were actually sunk. The mere presence of aircraft forced the submarines to submerge through fear of attack. Denied surface running to make use of their maximum speed and keep their batteries fully charged, the U-boats' radius of action and ability to locate targets were severely restricted. The Royal Navy Blimps were also useful for this purpose. Blimps, small non-rigid airships introduced into service in the summer of 1915, could be spotted up to ten miles away by an alert submarine lookout. Thus the Blimp was often able to act as a deterrent without actually spotting its target, the latter only being visible some five miles from the Blimp. From September 1916 Blimps based at Pulham St Mary regularly patrolled the East Coast. The notion of deterrence was taken one step further by the employment of lightly armed trainers, such as the AirCo. D.H.6, which were known as 'Scarecrows' and relied on the probability that U-boat commanders would submerge to avoid attack long before they could positively identify the actual type of patrolling aircraft. 'Scarecrow' patrols were flown from the end of 1917 when the U-boats began to concentrate on coastal merchantmen. The reason for this change in German tactics was the gradual introduction of the convoy system from May 1917. This was almost certainly the most important factor in successfully combatting the U-boat menace. Not only did convoys remove the constant stream of lone potential targets from the well known shipping lanes it also facilitated the better employment of both seaborne and airborne escorts.

Though flying air patrols might seem a rather mundane affair it was not without its dangers. Navigation over water was by dead reckoning, with suitable adjustments hopefully being made by guessing the strength and direction of the wind by studying the surface of the sea. Even when fitted with wireless, silence had to be maintained more than sixty miles from the coast for fear of announcing the presence of the patrolling aircraft to the enemy. Particularly early in the war, when engines were notoriously unreliable, there was always the possibility of a forced landing. In rough seas this could prove disastrous, and even if a successful landing was achieved running repairs would still have to be affected by the aircrew. The chances of rescue were small due to the large size of the patrol area, and the fact that it often included minefields. There was also the constant danger of enemy action, principally from the seaplane bases on the Belgian coast at Zeebrugge and Ostend. The German seaplanes, particularly the Hansa-Brandenburgs, were generally superior in performance to their British counterparts. The Curtiss H-12 and Felixstowe F2A flying boats were generally considered to be more than capable of flying offensive patrols against the German seaplanes, and it was not unknown for the former to use repeated wireless transmissions to attract the Germans. One such occasion when this ruse was used was on 4 June 1918 when five British flying boats engaged a number of German seaplanes, claiming six destroyed for the loss of a single flying boat.

The utilisation of the products of the new technology during the Great War did not prove Northcliffe's assertion in a purely physical sense. The English Channel, patrolled by the Royal Navy, remained Britain's essential defence; as arguably it still does today. What the Great War did prove was that Britain was 'no longer an island' in that its inhabitants had been denied the ability to isolate themselves from the affairs of mainland Europe. The new technology did not prevent war as the Wright Brothers had hoped, as the atom bomb scientists were to hope, instead it created a phenomenon known as the 'Home Front'. This was the first step towards the notion of 'Total War', though, fortunately, the Great War did not last long enough for the British to appreciate the full extent of this development of the means of waging war. The new technology undeniably changed the nature of warfare, but not one of its products was able to ensure domination. While technology is progressing it will constantly achieve mastery of its products; thus the development of radar would locate the bomber, and the development of the bomber will elude the radar.

During the 'Great War For Civilisation' it was the lot of the people of Norfolk and Suffolk to stoically endure the destructiveness of the products of the new technology. Though preparations to bomb Berlin were being made at Bircham Newton in 1918, nearly a quarter of a century was to pass before the reciprocal journey was made. Technology had progressed, Man had not.

Attleborough in the Great War

by
Philip Bujak

The war effort of a nation is usually measured in terms of statistics, in scales of millions rather than hundreds, armies as opposed to detachments and large cities but rarely villages. That this is so is understandable for a number of reasons. Time, it is often said, is a great healer. Memories are erased sometimes because they are short but more often because they are best forgotten. As the end of the twentieth century approaches only few remain who are able and willing to recount their own special memories of the 1914–18 conflict. As a consequence, discussion and examination of the effects of this war on the local community is rare, as is evidence other than eye-witness accounts. In analysis of the role of Attleborough in Norfolk, however, some of these obstacles have been overcome by a combination of new hitherto unpublished material in combination with a rejuvination of a most original and rare contemporary commentary on the effects of the war on the town.

Attleborough is one of the older market towns in East Anglia. In 1914 it had a number of attractive features that indicates that it was a well established community. A Co-operative society, millers, agricultural engineers, a foundry supplying agricultural machinery, motor mechanics and the town's largest single employer the Gaymers Cider Works. To underline Attleborough's links with agriculture there was also a Corn Hall located on Exchange Street that was a commercial focus for many of the surrounding farms. The town provided employment and other services in a way that would have made it a considerable centre for the surrounding population.

In 1919 the London and Norwich Press Ltd., printed a limited edition of a book written by Major J. H. Kennedy entitled *Attleborough in War Time – with a short Concurrent History of the Great War*. It is a rare collection of assorted evidence that gives a first hand account of the life of the town during the four years of the Great War. The second half of the book not only provides a detailed breakdown of the units, location and fate of the town's fighting men but also has a twenty page chronicle of the various stages of the conflict. This must have been one of the very first such narratives that would answer some of the questions of an often confused and frustrated civilian population who wondered why their men had died in Turkish prison camps or were killed in battles with curious sounding names that had become all too familiar over the previous four years.

But this book is not just a remarkably detailed record of where and how Attleborough men fought. One is also privy to the life of the town and the reaction of the townspeople to war. To some of the older residents the account is not unknown, having been passed down as a kind of sacred record of the life of the town through one of its most testing times. Major Kennedy too is still remembered by some of those who were children at the outbreak of war. As a regular Army Officer with over eleven years service, he was posted to command the 4th (Volunteer) Battalion of the Norfolk Regiment before moving under direct War Office control as Recruiting Officer for the Attleborough district. Without him this account of a town at war would be hard to produce in any detail, although it does have to be seen in the context of the time and some remarks should be treated with some circumspection. In a straightforward style Kennedy paints a picture of one town at war, which in many ways can be seen as representative of thousands of others nearly seventy years ago. Attleborough was not alone in being taken completely by surprise by the declaration of war.

With the benefit of hindsight one can easily imagine that England had plenty of time to brace itself for the possibility of war breaking out. The Archduke Franz Ferdinand of Austria had been assassinated on 28 June 1914. One month later no war had occurred although the national press had chronicled the mounting tension in Europe. But on the local level war still seemed most unlikely. Indeed the realities of the ensuing great power confrontation were still not widely known as is testified by a meeting held at Queen's Square in the centre of the town on 31 July. It was a sultry summer's day just before the Bank Holiday was to begin. The town was not empty but some had already left by rail for Yarmouth while others were settling into a routine for a few days rest from work. For the small crowd around a temporary platform the important Bank Holiday issue was not the impending war with Germany but Home Rule for Ireland! Throughout the nineteenth century politicians had been grappling with the Irish problem which in essence was the question of what should happen to the Protestant north, known as Ulster, should the south be given its independence from British rule. With the Curragh Mutiny at the end of 1913, where 57 out of 70 officers of a regiment in Ireland preferred dismissal to the possibility of fighting Ulstermen, the Liberal Government was facing disaster. By mid July 1914 Ireland was poised on the brink of civil war thus the town meeting can be seen against a background of a very serious domestic issue. Being very nearly harvest time too there were already many things to think about and events in Europe had gone largely unnoticed. After a short speech on the Irish situation another speaker mounted the platform to announce there was grave danger of a European war breaking out at any moment. The gravity of the situation had to be explained to the audience who had at first ridiculed the idea. Afterwards however many returned to their homes suddenly very much aware of a far more serious situation than that which they had hoped to hear of at the town square. Five days later Britain was at war. Reactions varied within the town. The overriding sentiment was one of intense patriotism, to outwardly show reservation or condemnation was ill-advised. Over thirty men from the town were already in uniform. Service in the Army was one way of avoiding unemployment or a life in agriculture, while six men were also serving in the Royal Navy when war was declared.[1] The last war that had seen townsmen fighting for their country had been the Boer War in South Africa, a localised conflict that had had a limited impact on Attleborough. But this was to be a world war, different from any previous experience that the town had ever known. Anglo-German rivalry was not a new phenomenon, with its origins as far back as 1890, and with the culmination of this in war it was seen as a great opportunity for adventure. In the first five months 145 men from the town enlisted for service. Others who had retired such as Sergeant Major B. Dickerson, who had 21 years previous service re-enlisted in September 1914.[2] On 5 August, the day after the British Government's declaration of war, Private P. J. Forster, with eleven years previous service re-enlisted with the 3rd Norfolk Regiment once more and soon found himself fighting and wounded on the River Aisne trying to hold back the advancing German troops who were pouring through Belgium. That the war would be over by Christmas had been a popular catchphrase to begin with but with the British Expeditionary Force falling back to the Marne and the increasing flow of casualities arriving at ports on the south coast this was soon to change. Just over eight weeks after he had enlisted Private Forster died of his wounds at a hospital in Brighton and was buried with full military honours, being one of the first fatalities, as the newspaper report recalls:

A HERO OF THE 1ST NORFOLKS
ATTLEBOROUGH MAN'S FUNERAL
Military honours at Brighton

The funeral of Private Philip James Forster, of the 1st Norfolk Regiment, who died at the 2nd Eastern General Hospital, Brighton, last Thursday from wounds received during the fierce fighting at the Aisne, took place with full military honours at the Extra Mural Cemetery, Brighton, on Monday.

The deceased soldier had only arrived home with 130 wounded on the previous Monday, and was constantly visited by a Norfolk lady living in Brighton. He was suffering from a bullet wound in the eye, that had caused a slight fracture of the skull, and although an operation was performed, he succumbed to his injuries on the Thursday. He was one of the four soldier sons of Mrs Forster, of Miller's Square, Attleborough, who received the news of Private Forster's serious condition exactly seven weeks from the day she said good-bye to him when the regiment left Norwich to join the First Expeditionary Force bound for the seat of war.

The funeral, which was solemnised in conjunction with that of a comrade in arms of the Highland Light Infantry, was a very impressive event, the bodies of the two soldiers being conveyed on gun carriages drawn by a gun team supplied by the Cadet Battalion of the St Peter's and St Nicholas Church Lads Brigade, while the bearers were drawn from the Ambulance Corps of the R.A.M.C. under the command of Major Booth, who with Lieutenant Walker and Lieutenant Ross marched in the long procession to the Cemetery. The Band of the Royal Field Artillery (T) headed the cortege, and performed Chopin's 'Funeral March' and Handel's 'Dead March in Saul', thousands of sympathetic spectators gathering all along the route from the hospital to Cemetery, where the Rev. Canon Hoskyns, Vicar of Brighton, performed the last sad rite, and the two soldiers were buried side by side.

As the coffins, of polished elm, with handsome brass fittings, were lowered into their last resting place a firing party of the 6th Cyclist Battalion, Royal Sussex Regiment (Hove), fired the farewell volleys over the grave, and the 'Last Post' was sounded by Bugler Virgo, R.A.M.C.

The chief mourners at Private Forster's funeral were his mother, four sisters, and two brothers, his nephew, Mr Fred Halstead and his brother-in-law, Mr Fred Smith. Lovely floral tributes were sent by his mother and sorrowing family, and from members of the Parkinsville Club, Belton, Durham, while Mr and Mrs Russell Coggs, late of Watton sent a wreath inscribed 'In memory of a brave East Anglian'.

In the next bed to Private Forster in the Star Ward of the Hospital where he died was Private Hunter, of the Queen's Royal West Surrey Regiment, who received his discharge on Monday, and has returned to his home at North Quay, Yarmouth.

The impact on the town of so many of its men going to fight, mostly in France, but in many other areas also, was immense. A very small number of residents can still remember the day when the largest group left the railway station after being checked in by a recruiting sergeant and seen off by the town's dignitories including Mr William Gaymer, owner of the Cider Factory, and the town's largest employer. The recruiting office was opened on 12 August to channel recruits into 'Kitchener's Army' – the 4th Norfolk Regiment being the main recipient of Attleborough's men in the early days.

To many of the men lined up on the platform the war was to be an adventure. An opportunity to serve King and Country, perhaps make a name for themselves and to return in uniform a hero. For others it was the only thing to do. Friends and relatives were joining or had already done so. Society expected the eligible men to go, not to, would be an impossible task. For some the next few months and years would mean wounds and medals, for others mud and a horrific death in some far off battlefield in Europe, Gallipoli or at sea. Some of Major Kennedy's 'Remarks' tell us what happened to some of these men sitting on Attleborough Station that August.[3] The town looked to its most prominent members for leadership. One of the most pressing concerns was the threat of invasion from Belgium or northern France. By mid August a force of thirty-five men had placed themselves at the disposal of Major Kennedy and they now patrolled the main roads at night, especially the Norwich to Newmarket route, and checked telegraph wires for sabotage. During the day this was performed by the local Boy Scouts, some on bicycles. One of the first efforts made by the whole town was a response to a call for temporary hospitals to receive wounded.

On 8 August the Town Hall was lent, free of any charges, until 31 December as a temporary hospital, one of many such events that occurred throughout the country. Plans for this type of emergency went back to 1911 when the Attleborough District of the Red Cross Society was founded. It was these ladies, certificated in First Aid, that first staffed the sixteen bed Auxiliary Hospital with a cooking area and reception room to augment the ward.

The first sick and wounded arrived in late November from the Norfolk and Norwich Hospital which was the main recipient of troops from London. Local people were involved with the hospital in a variety of ways. To many it was the only way they felt they could actively contribute to the war effort. Many of the food supplies were donated on a daily basis. Gifts of fruit, vegetables, cakes, tobacco and even pheasants would be brought in from time to time and the first Christmas of the war saw an evening carol service at the hospital.

If there was one year during the conflict however when the war seemed to overshadow all else it was 1915. A new National Ministry had been formed in London to organise the nation's resources more effectively. It was clear that Lord Kitchener's view that the conflict could go on for three years might well be correct and if that was so then tighter controls were needed.[4] One of the first results was the beginning of the National Thrift Campaign. Wages had been rising too fast – even those of agricultural labourers, while enemy submarine action was accelerating the problems of shortages. A Vegetable Products Committee was set up in the town, which sat at Point House in Church Street, and the town community brought along what they could spare. Parcels were then put together, a few re-distributed to those in hardship in the town, while the majority were despatched to warships anchored off the east coast; H.M.S. *Rose* and H.M.S. *Esther* both thanked the town for their gifts.

The degeneration of the very mobile nature of the war, in its earlier stages, into trench warfare and stalemate meant that an end to the conflict seemed a long way off. On 5 August 1915 National Registration Day was held and all the names of men between the ages of 15 and 50 were placed on a register. On 14 and 15 August South Norfolk was visited by Zeppelins on their way to London.

By the end of the summer of 1915, 95% of the original British Expeditionary Force of regular and Territorial Units, sent to France in August the previous year, were either dead, wounded or missing. The demand for men continued. Men from the town had been fighting in some of the most infamous battles of the war, for example Ypres where Sergeant G. E. Briggs had been wounded on 23 April 1915, Private F. E. Crummett of the 7th Norfolks had been killed in October in Flanders, Sergeant Fisher of the 1st Northamptonshire Regiment was wounded at the Aisne on 17 September 1914 as was Private P. J. Forster who was mentioned earlier. But then a new name, far from Flanders, began to claim the lives of more Attleborough men – Gallipoli.

Heavy losses here continued through to January 1916 and a steady stream of War Office telegrams reached out into the provinces, some destined for families in Attleborough. August was a bad month. On 12 August 1915, Sergeant John Dye and Private Albert Shaw of the 4th Norfolks were both killed in action at Gallipoli. Three days later Private Charles Lincoln was drowned when H.M.S. *Royal Edward* sank in the Dardanelles to be followed on 2 September by Private Robert Shaw also of the 4th Norfolks who died 3 weeks after his brother. They had both enlisted on the same day in 1914.

Recruiting continued unabated in 1915. Norfolk was divided into sections and Attleborough became the headquarters of the largest of these which included many towns that had already given up thousands of their men to the various county regiments and corps of the Army. According to Major Kennedy, who had recently been appointed Recruiting Officer for the district, Norfolk had been one of the three most 'patriotic' counties under the voluntary system with 770 men having passed through the Attleborough office alone by September 1914.

Meanwhile an active social life had developed around the Auxiliary Hospital. In June 1915 the number of beds had been increased to twenty-three and on 2 August the staff and patients were joined by their counterparts from the many other similar hospitals in the area at a sport and entertainment afternoon held at the nearby grounds of Old Buckenham

Hall. Croquet, bowls and many other events were arranged for the patients and Attleborough could boast two champions and local men at that!

The year 1916 saw no let up in the demands made on the town nor an end to the war. Keeping the morale of the townspeople going was always a major problem. So far the majority had played a significant part, as far as they could. The Compulsory Service Bill however increased the every day problems faced by families operating without fathers, sons and friends. All unmarried men between the ages of 18 and 41 were now called into the armed forces. In May the Military Service Act enlisted all married men of military age. The printing firm of Johnson Bros. whose premises backed onto the town Drill Hall were forced to close as all its employees were called up. Consequently there were very few able bodied men left to defend the town in case of invasion, which was still felt to be possible. A company of the Voluntary Training Corps was founded, and similar units training Cadets at some local schools followed. They were led by Major Kennedy and had a strength of about forty men; this later was expanded to a battalion sized unit based at Wymondham. The men that made up this unit tended to be beyond service age or deemed medically unfit for active service overseas.

The country had been drained of its first line manpower for a purpose. On 1 July 1916 the Somme battle began. For many in the town it was thought that this would be the beginning of the end of the war. Vast amounts of men and ammunition had been prepared and a five day bombardment preceded the attack which included various units of the Norfolk Regiment. The battle is painted by Major Kennedy as a determined and generally successful offensive in *Attleborough at War*, with 'ground being gained every day' and he was certain that the German front would undoubtedly have been broken had the weather not deteriorated in October.[5] That the battle is not covered in more detail is understandable, it would take many years before the full horrors of this part of the war became widely known. It was sufficient to see the British Army playing its glorious part in defeating the 'hun'. More Attleborough men fell at this stage including Private Ernest R. Elvin of the 8th Norfolks, who had enlisted in August 1914, who was killed in action at Delville Wood on 19 July 1916.

In the autumn of 1916 a new ministerial department was formed to be known as the Ministry of National Service. The War Office, once led by Lord Kitchener who had lost his life aboard H.M.S. *Hampshire* on 5 June, now relinquished control of recruiting. The local Recruiting Office now moved from Major Kennedy's home, Attleborough Lodge, to the Royal Hotel in the centre of the town. A staff of twenty-seven clerks alone worked from the hotel but one wonders where the recruits were going to come from. By the time conscription had been introduced 5,041,000 men had volunteered for service and Attleborough with its pre-war population of approximately 2,500 had already put 400 men into uniform!

Aerial bombing raids did not come on the same scale as they did 25 years later, but the sight of an airship, or Zeppelin, roaming the skies above East Anglia was a frightening one for many. In December 1915 a lighting order had been issued restricting vehicles on the roads at night unless they had both a pass and shaded lamps. In January 1916 Swaffham was bombed, five people had already been killed in raids on Dereham, and on 31 July it was Attleborough's turn although no damage was done. Norwich escaped raids it was thought at the time because the Kaiser had planned to make it his headquarters after the invasion.

By 1917 there were real shortages of sugar, flour, potatoes and many other foodstuffs. Although there was no national rationing system it was encouraged at a local level and on a voluntary basis. The hitherto uncompromising praise of the townspeople by Major Kennedy now starts to give way as the strain of war began to tell on everyone. On 23 August sugar was rationed for the first time and was soon followed by bacon, jam, meat and butter before the end of July. Children too felt the effects of war as sweets became scarce, as did the money with which to buy them.

In April 1917 the Wayland Infirmary, a small local hospital two miles north of the town, was taken over by the War Office. With over 100 beds it overshadowed its auxiliary counterpart in the town and in November the Auxiliary Hospital was closed. To many residents of the town the hospital had been a place where they could 'do their bit' for the troops and in the three years that it was opened £782.6s.3d. was contributed by local people for its upkeep. It was with great annoyance and frustration that the committee responsible for the running of the hospital, including Mrs Kennedy who was the commandant, received the War Office explanation that the building was not 'structurally suitable for a hospital', although of course at one time they had thought otherwise. So ended the town hospital. In three years it had treated 656 patients, provided concerts and transport and had three of the staff mentioned in despatches.[6] By April 1919 the Wayland Infirmary would have treated a further 997 patients.

But there were still other ways to help the war effort. The Norwich War Hospital Supply Depot relied on local collectors to provide ward garments, bandages and many other smaller items which would be passed on to hospitals in Great Britain or abroad which lacked many basic necessities. A total of 18,434 articles were passed on to the Association from the Attleborough branch which was again staffed by female volunteers.[7] The cost of the war could not be borne through taxation alone so War Savings Associations were formed. Female collectors issued coupons from March 1917 onwards which were purchased from the Government instead of

L3 the Zeppelin which bombed Great Yarmouth, 19 January 1915 (J. Provan)

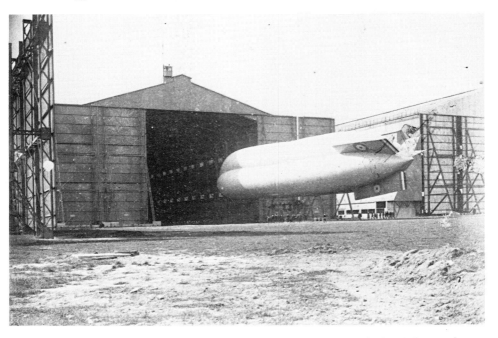

Coastal Class 'Blimp' at Pulham (Norfolk & Suffolk Aviation Museum)

St Peter's Villa, St Peter's Plain, Great Yarmouth. Damage caused by the same bombs which killed two people in January 1915 (Nicholas Forder)

Curtiss Flying Boat H.12 B 'N4332' – delivered from January 1918, R.N.A.S. Great Yarmouth (J. M. Bruce/G. S. Leslie)

Boulton & Paul Bobolink (J. M. Bruce/G. S. Leslie)

D.H.4s, D.H.9 and B.E.2 R.N.A.S. Great Yarmouth, 1917/1918. D.H.9 '01654'
built by Mann Egerton (Norwich) (Peter Liddle)

B.E.2c '8626', the aircraft flown by Flt. Sub-Lieut. E. L. Pulling when engaging
with Zeppelin L-21 in November 1916. Pulling was later killed in the same aircraft
when it broke up in the air when looping the loop on 2 March 1917 (P. Wright)

Volunteers at Attleborough Station ready to leave, August 1914

Norwich Recruits, Guildhall Hill, Norwich, 1914 (Norwich Central Library 1999)

Volunteers at Mulbarton and Swardeston, 1914 (NCL W 26352)

Essex Regiment in Norwich Market Place, August 1914 (NCL W 1996)

Essex Regiment having haircut August 1914 (NCL 1998)

Carrow Works Clubhouse, Norwich, 1914 (NCL 1994)

Liquid refreshment for the Army (NCL W 2004)

Officers of the 1/2 Norfolk R.F.A. Battery, 26 May 1915 (NCL 2120)

Norfolk Tribunal (NCL W 2563)

Naval Recruiting day, July 1915 (NCL W 2655)

Captured German gun, 1916, being shown to the Mayor of Norwich Sir G. Chamberlin (NCL W 2657)

Lucy Bignold making a speech for Norwich Tank Week, 1 to 6 April 1916 (NCL W 2598)

Norwich Tank Week – Tank departs (NCL W 2592)

Presentation of medals in the Market Place, Norwich in 1919, by Major Gen. Sir
J. E. Capper, K.C.B. (NCL W 2651)

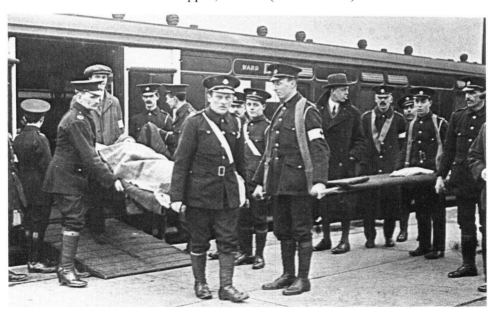

Norwich Division of the Red Cross unloading the wounded at Thorpe Station,
Norwich (NCL W 2935)

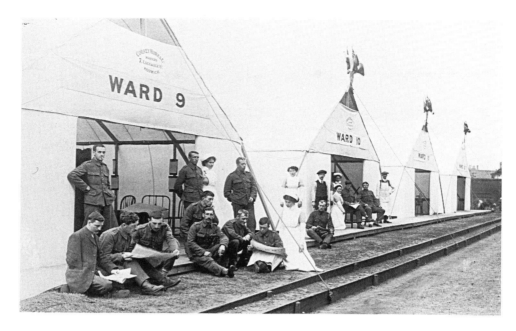

First annex ward in a Norfolk War Hospital (NCL W 2646)

Y.M.C.A. entertaining the wounded, 1916 (NCL W 2653)

A military funeral (NCL 1992)

George Edwards with a copy of his book 'From Crowscaring to Westminster'
probably taken on publication day in 1922 (Noel Edwards)

Armistice Day, Norwich, 1918 (NCL 2656)

investment in the Post Office and steady rather than spectacular progress was made throughout 1917 and 1918.

The harvest of 1917 was in serious danger of being lost for want of labour. However in common with many other farming areas school children were marshalled to the areas of greatest need to help with harvesting badly needed grain. For Attleborough this meant the arrival of boys from two of the most prestigious public schools at that time, Downing College, Bath and Sherborne School. With labour exceptionally short these extra hands were invaluable.

News from the front in France arrived regularly in the provincial press and now the hope was for victory at Ypres on the Franco–Belgian border. The sound of gunfire was not just audible on the south coast but in Norfolk too as Sir Douglas Haig launched his next offensive on the last day of July. But again our lack of success was, according to Major Kennedy, due to the almost continuous rain. But the men from the town were far from disgracing themselves. By the end of 1917 at least three Military Medal and two Military Cross awards had been made to servicemen from the town. By the end of the war this list would be even longer.

News of the revolution in Russia was a blow as the Russian Army now withdrew from the conflict. With rationing and food economy lectures in December the Christmas of 1917 was a bleak time. The best Christmas present of all it seems was for the postman not to call. Every card that arrived to a family with a close relative serving abroad caused anguish followed hopefully by relief. Attitudes towards the war had changed enormously by the start of 1918.

Efforts to maintain a spirit of patriotism and determination continued but the zest for defeating the enemy had certainly subsided. The entry of the United States into the war would certainly ease the pressure on the allied armies but the losses continued, especially following the new and last desperate German offensive that began at Cambrai in late March. On 10 April the maximum age limit for active service was raised to fifty and many legal exemptions that had saved many from joining were abolished. By this stage Attleborough, like everywhere else had exhausted its supply of manpower. One hundred and five men had joined up from Gaymer's Cider Works alone by 1918. A measure of the nearly desperate situation is the fact that Parliament granted special powers in order to apply Compulsory Service to Ireland.

As the tide of the war turned against the Germans during the summer of 1918 so domestic political frustrations once more raised their heads. Four years of war had left numerous social and political issues in a state of suspended animation, much to the relief of Asquith's Government of 1914. To Major Kennedy the police strike of August and the general strike on the railways late in the same month were the actions of unpatriotic workers stirred into action by the same people who were now claiming that the Government would not be able to pay back War Savings money. Events in Europe unfolded quickly. November 1918 saw the collapse of German resistance, a revolt in Berlin by the communists and the abdication of the Kaiser on the 9th. The German army had been eventually defeated but 'utterly vanquished and hopelessly disorganised', was not as Major Kennedy saw it, yet that is the way perhaps it had to be seen.[8] One week before the armistice was signed on 11 November Private H. R. W. Rudd was killed by a shell explosion in France. Rudd was the last Attleborough man to be killed in action but two more were to die in December, Private Speck of his wounds and Corporal W. F. Rayner in Turkish captivity. Both men had been regular soldiers with twenty-eight years previous service between them.

It took some time for many of the surviving men to return to the town. For some it was a hero's welcome while others who had not died in battle as far as is known never returned at all. Altogether Attleborough had provided 550 men to the service of the nation, one-fifth of the total population. Ninety-seven of these were killed or missing in action. Eleven Attleborough women also joined the Land Army or equivalent organisations.[9] In more than one sense every man or woman that fought was a hero and many more brave deeds were performed than received recognition by the award of a medal. Nevertheless a total of nine Military Medals and four Military Crosses were presented, some post-humously, to men from Attleborough, a record that the town can always feel justifiably proud of.

> (Wounded and gassed) Cpl. H. R. Barber was awarded the Military Medal in 1916
> (Wounded at Ypres) Sgt. G. E. Briggs was awarded the Military Medal in 1916
> (K.I.A. 22.9.18) Capt. T. A. K. Cubitt was awarded the Military Cross (11.10.17)
> (Gassed and wounded twice) Cpl. H. W. Eagling was awarded the Military Medal
> Pte. W. S. Dorling was awarded the Military Medal
> Lt. G. D. Greenland was awarded the Military Cross
> Maj. R. M. Jacob was awarded the Military Cross in 1917
> L/Cpl. M. Leeder was awarded the Military Medal
> (Wounded and gassed) Lt. H. S. Ling was awarded the Military Cross
> (Wounded arm and leg) Sgt. Leonard Littleproud was awarded the Military Medal
> Cpl. A. E. Myhill was awarded the Military Medal in Palestine

(Died of wounds 6.4.17) Pte. H. Stephenson was awarded the Military Medal

(Died a prisoner of war 1.11.18) Cpl. W. J. Sturman was awarded the Military Medal

The enormous casualty roll made it impossible to bring home the bodies of those killed. Instead they were interred in official war graves. For those with the time or inclination these places never fail to stun and mystify the visitor. To walk endlessly through rows of gleaming white gravestones each with some inscription and often regimental badges carved into it is an awe-inspiring sight. Yet somewhere out there are the graves of many of the ninety-seven Attleborough casualties. Not many perhaps compared to the thousands suffered by other towns or cities, but each one a member of a community that knew them briefly and saw them no more. But it did remember them. The national memorial of the Cenotaph was the focus for the national grief but thousands of communities needed far more than that. At the junction of Exchange and Church Streets the town's own memorial was dedicated on 27 June 1920. Gaymer's Cider too placed their own plaque within their factory walls to their eight men who never returned. In St Mary's Church a brass wall plate was erected by the family of Gunner Bertie Ponder of the Machine Gun Corps a timeless puzzle to generations of young children driven, by some less than inspirational sermon, to reading the inscription and studying the crossed machine guns. But such is the case all over the nation. Very soon even those that were children at the time of this great conflict will be gone and the stone memorial will contain but names of a generation that present townspeople never knew and whose contribution to the town was so prematurely ended.

Notes

A Note on Sources
The factual material used has been compiled from three main areas. The
first edition of *Attleborough in Wartime* by Major J. H. Kennedy
provides the base of the chapter. Further explanation and material is
provided by present residents of the town coupled with the author's
research into archival material held at the Norwich, Brighton and
National Libraries as well as at the Regimental Museum, Norwich.

1. The following men were already serving prior to August 1914.

Cpl. Barber, H. R.	M.M. 1916
Barker, A. P.	C.S.M.
Beck, F.	P.O. R.N. (K.I.A.)
Bird, J.	Pte.
Blaxall, A. B.	R.N.
Briggs, G. E.	Sgt. M.M.
Clarke, A. G.	C.O.S. R.N.
Clarke, C. F.	R.S.M. 1st Norf. Regt.
Clarke, E. A.	Pte. R.A.M.C./R.E.
Cocking, F. W.	L/cpl. 6th Norf. Regt.
Daynes, A.	Pte. 1st Norf. Regt. (DOW)
Fincham, T.	Pte. 1st Yorks. Regt. (14 years previous service DOW 2.6.17)
Fisher, W.	Sgt.
George, S. J.	Pte.
George, W. G.	Pte. 1st East Kent
Griffin, F. K.	1st Norf. Regt.
2 Lt. Hillier, F. W.	
Hunt, A. S. S.	R.F.A. (DOW 5.10.18)
Maj. Jacob, R. M.	130th K.G.O. M.C.
Key, J. W.	P.O. R.N.
Kingdom, J. A.	Sgt.
Landsdell, F. J.	Pte. 2nd Norf. Regt.
Mann, H.	L/cpl.
Parker, S.	Pte.
Patrick, A.	Pte. 2nd Norf. Regt. (DOW 15.4.16)
Peters, A. R.	
Potter, A. W. R.	Sgt. 2nd Norf. Regt.
Pratt, A. S.	R.N.
Pratt, V. J.	Pte. 1/4th Norfolk (KIA 2.11.17)
Rayner, G. A.	L/cpl. 2nd Norf. Regt. (DIA 1916)
Redit, G.	R.H.A.

Redit, J.	R.F.A. (KIA)
Reeve, A.	L/cpl. 2nd Norf. Regt.
Sharman, F. P.	L.S. R.N.
Sharman, W. A.	P.O. R.N.
Standley, E. J.	Sgt. 19th Hussars
Stumen, W.	Pte. 3rd Norf. Regt.
Temple, A. J.	Pte. Gren. Guards
Tillot, L. W.	R.A.M.C. Pte.
Webster, G. W.	Cpl. R.F.A.
Webster, W. R.	Sgt. R.F.A. (KIA 12.5.15)
Woodrow, S. D.	Cpl. 6th Norf. Regt.

2. He survived the war and was demobilised 7.10.17.
3. The following is a sample of men who enlisted between August and November 1914:

Ayton, Mathew, Pte. (En. 8.10.14) 6th Norfolks. Wounded, left leg amputated.

Banyard, George (En. 6.8.14) 4th Norfolks. Wounded neck and shoulder, Gaza, 19.4.17.

Barnard, Bertie, Cpl. (En. 10.9.14) 2/4th Norfolks. KIA 14.4.17.

Briggs, Elijah Samuel, Pte. (En. 10.8.14) W. Yorks. KIA 1.7.16.

Dunnett, George, Pte. (En. 10.9.14) 2/4th Norfolks. Gassed 11.5.18.

Fincham, William, L/cpl. (En. 3.9.14) 3rd Norfolks. DOW 2.6.17.

Gutteridge, Herbert, Pte. (En. 20.11.14) 7th Norfolks. Shell shock, wounded right hand. Gassed.

Lincoln, Charles, Pte. (En. 10.14) 4th Norfolks. Drowned at sea 15.8.15.

Pinnock, Archie, Pte. (En. 10.9.14) 2/4th Norfolks. Wounded, back, chest and stomach.

Sharpe, Cecil G., Pte. (En. 4.8.14) 1/4th Norfolks. Wounded in chest bursting shell, buried at sea.

Smith, George W., Pte. (En. 4.8.14) 9th Norfolks. KIA Delville Wood 15.9.16.

Sparrow, Charles (En. 6.8.14) 1/4th Norfolks Gallipoli. Wounded and mentioned in despatches.

4. Lord Kitchener's view was largely disregarded at this time. See *August 1914* by Barbara Tuchman (Papermac).
5. J.H.K., p. 42.
6. Mrs J. H. Kennedy, Mrs W. Greenland, Mrs G. Keeling.
7. Mrs Rose, Mrs Jones, Miss Robinson.
8. J.H.K., p. 62.
9. J.H.K., p. 114. *Women who served:*

Clements, Dorothy R., Clerk Q.M.A.A.C., July 1918 to November 1918.

Clements, Eva E., Land Army, July 1915. Good Conduct and Long Service Badges and 2 Stripes.

Downes, Florence, Clerk in W.R.A.F., March 1919.

Fisher, Agnes, Land Army, 22 April 1918. Good Conduct Badge and 3 Stripes.

Fisher, Daisy, Land Army, 7 June 1918. Good Conduct Badge and 3 Stripes.

Fisher, Lily, Land Army, 7 June 1918. Good Conduct Badge and 3 Stripes.

Houchen, F. V. (Mrs), Q.M.A.A.C., as Administrator, September 1916 to February 1919.

Lincoln, Minnie, N.A.C.B. 1918.

Parker, Alice, Land Army, 13 September to December 1918.

Parker, Jessie K. I., Land Army, 15 May 1917 to 13 February 1919. Obtained Land Army Badge and Good Service Badge.

Seggar, Olive H., joined N.A.C.B., 8 May 1919.

Norwich: 1914–18

by

Peter Kent

The Great War changed Norwich from a cathedral city with agricultural industries into a large military centre with factories turning over to making a range of military hardware from shell cases to fighter planes – and even the furry boots of the men who flew them.

Thousands of troops in the khaki of the fit and the light blue of the convalescent filled the streets: many were training at Britannia Barracks before being sent to the Front and most of these were billeted in city homes.

At night citizens stumbled about the streets in dread of attack from the air in a city darkened on the order of a government that also demanded that the pubs be shut at 9.30 p.m., that food be rationed, labour directed, and income tax raised to the unheard of heights of six shillings in the pound.

Although there was no physical damage – not a single bomb hit the city – the short-term social effects were widespread: unemployment almost disappeared, and women and girls abandoned their traditional domestic occupations to operate lathes and typewriters; traditional sexual morality was undermined, prompting a letter of outrage to the Lord Mayor from over 60 solid citizens; even the school day was shortened, and teachers put to work winding bandages.

Change did not come suddenly; indeed for the first few months life in many respects went on as before. But the outbreak of war had not come as a complete surprise: the international crisis had been ominously rumbling in the background since the assassination of the Archduke Franz Ferdinand of Austria in June 1914 and the news from Europe had been daily growing worse.

On 1 August it was learned that Russia had mobilised and Lord Kitchener had been summoned to give counsel to the King. The following day, as the troop trains began to roll all over Europe, prayers for peace were said in all the Norwich churches, and a small band of socialists met on the Cattle Market beneath the castle to protest against the inexorable slide into war raising their voices against 'the unscrupulous system of butchery and plunder engineered by the capitalists'.[1]

At midnight on 3 August 1914, the ultimatum given to the German

First Sunday morning parade of the City of Norwich Volunteers in Norwich Market Place, 1915 (NCL W 5173)

Leaving Norwich to enlist (NCL 1990)

government expired and Great Britain was at war. The following morning's *Eastern Daily Press* carried an appeal to all former soldiers, whether regular, volunteer or territorial, inviting them to join the 4th battalion of the Norfolk Regiment. All that day streams of men made their way up the hill to Britannia Barracks or to the drill hall at Chapelfield. R. H. Mottram, then a clerk at Bank Plain, went to Chapelfield with eight companions and enlisted. To his disappointment, instead of being given a rifle and uniform he had to be content with a red brassard, like a temporary postman, and was then sent home.[2]

Two train loads full of the 12th Lancers arrived at Thorpe Station and two hundred reservists left in a special train with much cheering and waving, an observer remarking that it was 'wonderful to see how happy were both the soldiers and their relatives'.[3] Over the next few days the city was full of unaccustomed military activity with plenty of opportunity to wave flags, cheer and press gifts upon the troops. The desire of the citizens to do this constituted the first of the many social problems of the war and the Lord Mayor was forced to appeal that they send money to his fund for the servicemen's families rather than jamming packets of cigarettes into the tunics of non-smokers.

Despite the peacetime presence of two barracks in the city – Britannia on Mousehold and Cavalry in Barrack Street – it was still a novelty for the citizens to see artillery rumbling through the streets and a surprise one day to see several hundred fully equipped troops settling down in the Market Place. A battalion of infantry had been stationed on the coast the previous weekend and had been withdrawn into the city. As the troops rested, local barbers brought out chairs and gave the men field service haircuts before a fascinated crowd who were just as interested in four German prisoners standing morosely within a ring of bayonets beneath the statue of the Duke of Wellington. There was some disappointment when they learned that the Germans were not part of the advance guard of the Kaiser's army but waiters who had been captured at Cromer; nonetheless a rumour soon spread that they had been tapping telegraph wires.[4]

A counter attraction to the troops in the Market Place were the new recruits drilling in Chapelfield Gardens. They had no weapons or uniforms and within a few days there were so many of them that their commanding officer was forced to appeal for one thousand pairs of boots as the government stores were exhausted. But many of the recruits did not leave their jobs immediately, and it was the prompt disappearance of the reservists that caused the most disruption to public services. Six of the police force left at once to rejoin their regiments and the tramway company was quite depleted with over twenty-five of its staff returning to the colours. The Post Office lost so many men that one of the first effects of the war was the restriction of postal deliveries from six to four a day.

It was not only men that disappeared: the gold sovereign was immediately withdrawn from circulation, and a wave of panic buying emptied the shops of groceries. The day after the declaration of war the International Stores sold more than it usually did in a week and was forced to place advertisements reassuring its customers that starvation was not imminent. There were those who took advantage of the fraught circumstances to overcharge and the public was warned of unscrupulous traders who sought to profiteer from bags of best siftings.

Despite all this activity there was at this stage no blackout and no sudden application of government regulations curtailing individual freedoms, although the *Norwich Mercury* did carry the following announcement:

'In common with other newspapers the *Norwich Mercury* has decided in view of the existing circumstances of national concern not to publish for the present any news concerning the movements of British troops or the deposition of our Naval forces, other than official information issued by the Admiralty and War Office.'[5]

Following this announcement, even innocuous photographs of soldiers marching through the streets or training gradually disappeared to be replaced by a weekly gallery of local men serving in the forces and those who had been killed. In the absence of any real information from the Front and the careful management of home news, rumours flourished: spies were everywhere, the Boy Scouts could hardly set out on patrol without coming across severed telegraph wires, pigeons were shot and found to be carrying coded messages, the night skies flashed with the lamps of secret German sympathisers, everyone knew someone who had seen trains full of Russians with snow on their boots and every concrete tennis court was seen as the artfully pre-prepared position of monster German siege artillery. Despite extraordinary vigilance, not a single German spy was discovered – but all knew that they were there, lurking and awaiting the moment to strike.

In response to public opinion, a fortnight after the outbreak of war all aliens were ordered to register with the police and were confined to within five miles of their home. There were about two hundred affected by the order in Norwich, mostly Italians, but with some Germans and Austrians. Aliens were subject to certain extra restrictions designed to reduce their potential as spies and saboteurs. They were forbidden to have guns or explosives, more than three gallons of any inflammable spirit, motor cars, motor bikes and pigeons. They had to hand over their cameras, any odd copy they might possess of military manuals or naval charts, their telephones were disconnected and they were expressly forbidden to have any code or 'means of conducting secret correspondence'. If enforced to the letter, this would have prevented them from having any milk or a copy of the *Pilgrim's Progress*.[6] This, however, was not enough to still public agitation against enemy aliens. Although there were no disgraceful incidents in Norwich of attacks on them or their property, the announcement in October that all Germans and Austrians between the ages of thirteen and forty-five were to be interned was greeted with general satisfaction.

All through the late summer and early autumn the pace of the war increased although recruiting efforts actually slackened and could not have been helped by a police ban on enlistment posters being fixed to lamposts and tramway standards.[7] The advertisement columns in the local newspapers showed little sign of a great demand for men; there were no full page advertisements appealing for recruits and, apart from a discreet insertion in the situations vacant column that called for 'good men and boys' between the ages of 15½ and 25 to join the Royal Navy, one would hardly have known that there was a war on; there was an appeal for a 'general wanted one mile from the city' but the qualifications needed there were domestic not martial.

After the initial rush of recruits the most obvious effect of the war was, paradoxically, the fear of unemployment. Industry had not then begun to turn to war production, and trade, particularly in inessential or luxury items, had decreased markedly. Norwich women were urged to buy the latest autumn fashions to prevent unemployment, probably the only time that self-indulgence has been seen as a patriotic and civic duty, and, as a temporary measure, a small workshop was set up for unemployed women to make soft toys and other fancy goods. It is a truism that the war liberated women from domestic service and lowly paid jobs by offering them better paid employment in the expanding war industries but this trend was slow to be seen in Norwich. Throughout the war the advertisements for domestic staff remained as numerous as ever, although the positions may not all have been filled.

As the lists of those killed, wounded or captured began to grow, the city adapted itself to the war and committees began to proliferate. There were Red Cross committees, soldiers' welfare committees, committees for the relief of Serbian refugees, salvaging waste materials and saving food. Flag days for all sorts of exotic causes became commonplace, women in cossack costume rattling tins on behalf of the Russians or in ordinary dress in aid of the more prosaic Belgians. Foreign delegates were regularly welcomed and the city became accustomed to the strains of unfamiliar anthems.

With letters from the Front came souvenirs, fragments of shell and photographs that were occasionally published in the local press if they did not infringe security. Herbert Duncan's hosiery shop in St Giles had the first display of captured trophies in the city; eight helmets, some bayonets and a fragment of the charred altar cloth of Ypres cathedral. This was soon eclipsed by a captured 77-mm field gun displayed in the Market Place.

The demands of the war effort gradually seeped into all aspects of the city's life. Even the 'Children's Corner' in the *Norwich Mercury* succumbed to martial fervour, Uncle Arthur regaling his young readers with patriotic stories of boys who wanted to be soldiers but were eventually content with joining the Boy Scouts. As a cunning device to accustom the city's children to paper rationing he instigated competitions to see how many words they could fit on to a postcard. The newsagents began to stock a range of publications solely devoted to the war; some were serious with lavish illustrations and careful articles, others quite ridiculous. One wonders just how many people could hardly wait for the next edition of the magazine *Answers* with its 'superb war romance of the Great War', 'A Place in the Sun'. Did they really thrill to read this piece of martial Mills and Boonery?

'Something in the cold sinister aspect of the cloaked figure, thrown into lurid relief by the flickering firelight: something in the imperious, arrogant tones of the voice suddenly caused Lucy Meadows to realise that she was in the presence of the Great Hun – the Kaiser William himself.'[8]

The ravages of the war on literature were to be even worse than this and Norwich's first published war poem makes 'A Place in the Sun' a model of restrained understatement. The poem, of which a single verse should suffice, was written by the wisely anonymous G.E.:

'He "cultured" and vultured poor Belgium at will,
He wolfed and he tigred till his prey lay quite still,
He tore out her vitals and drank her life stream,
Then gobbled the carcass with fiendish gleam.'[9]

'He' was, of course, the Great Hun – the Kaiser William, and shortly afterwards all were reassured to learn that he had been removed from the list of honorary admirals of the Royal Navy and was no longer a Knight of the Garter.

It seemed that it was only civilians that liked reading about the war. When the City Library was asked to report on soldiers' literary tastes it found that books on philosophy and religion were far more popular than tracts on the evils of Prussian militarism. 'Soldiers unlike civilians are comparatively indifferent to the literature on the Great War.'[10] William James' *The Varieties of Religious Experience* was particularly popular. The soldiers of the new army had rather more literary tastes than their pre-war counterparts and the reading room and reference library was always full. The Library Committee ordered local newspapers for the Scottish troops stationed in the city and took care to purchase books on subjects of national importance like munition making and guides to thrift and economy.[11]

The requests of servicemen at the Front, or in training camps, for comforts or even necessities that could not be met from official issues were slowly reflected in the goods on offer in the shops. It became possible to buy special hampers for the Front, 'battle belts', sleeping helmets and even khaki writing paper, while wool and knitting patterns for balaclavas and extra heavy socks were readily available.

Women were encouraged to knit or lavish attention on the few bewildered Belgian refugees who arrived in the city: but what was available to the patriotic men, who for reasons of age, health or family responsibilities, could not enlist and take their place in the firing line? There was a large body of such men all eager to help the war effort and various organisations quickly sprang up to utilise their good will. The war had hardly begun before an appeal went out to motorists to place their vehicles at the disposal of the authorities in the event of an invasion or similar emergency. Immediately two hundred motor cars and a similar number of motor-bikes were offered, and a list compiled of all those others that might be of use. An invasion committee was set up whose role was to plan routes of evacuation and services for refugees, while an emergency corps of twelve hundred men was recruited to keep the roads open and to undertake repairs. The ubiquitous Boy Scouts had their role in this organisation too: they were to act as 'callers', summoning the adults to their duties when the occasion demanded, while the Girl Guides proved their fieldcraft by mapping the tracks and lanes to provide alternative routes to the main roads.[12]

For those who wished to play a more martial role, a volunteer corps was formed in December 1914. The original Volunteers, raised in 1860 to provide a supplementary home defence force to the regular army, had been abolished and reconstituted as the Territorial Force. But this had been largely sent overseas as a reinforcement to the B.E.F. and all future recruitment was, at Kitchener's insistence, to the regular army only. This left large numbers of men too old for the army but fit enough to undertake lighter military duties at home who agitated to be allowed to be of use.

A meeting of all those interested in forming a new volunteer force was held in the Drill Hall on 19 December. Lieutenant-Colonel Leathes Prior was elected commanding officer and six hundred men joined at once what became known as the Norwich Volunteer Training Corps. They had no uniforms and no arms and the War Office at first wanted nothing to do with them. The official view was that their negligible military value was more than offset by the reprisals they would invite from the Germans who would certainly regard them as *franc-tireurs*. The volunteers persevered in the face of official indifference and a certain degree of local ridicule, route marching about the country lanes and drilling in Chapelfield Gardens, but it was difficult to win public confidence when they had no uniforms and pretended that umbrellas and walking sticks were rifles. The minimum age was thirty-eight – anyone younger could be expected to join the army – and the volunteers did not want to be seen as a soft option. By mid 1915 they had equipped themselves with fifty old Martini rifles, purchased grey uniforms, and formed a bugle band that led them on their marches.

The public continued to regard them with some amusement, but the 'Cripples Brigade' and 'England's Last Hope' went on training seriously. A miniature rifle range was set up in Mountergate, the use of Howard House in King Street was offered to them as a headquarters and most members trained twice a week in squads all over the city. At Easter, 1915, the corps paraded on Mousehold Heath, nearly eight hundred strong, and was inspected by Major-General Daniell, the local commanding officer of the regular troops, who seemed well pleased. Their role for the rest of the war was to be mundanely useful: they patrolled the railway lines and guarded bridges and each weekend a trainload was taken to Pulham Market to help in building the airship station where they dug out most of the trackbed for the railway line to the site. The social composition of the battalion was initially almost entirely of the middle and business classes but a more varied social mix was brought about with the introduction of conscription, when exemption from the army for those in reserved occupations was granted on condition they joined the volunteers.[13]

Those that felt that even amateur soldiering was beyond them but still wished to serve in an official capacity were urged to become special constables and by the end of 1914 nearly seven hundred had been sworn in. The reason for such a large number was because the regular police force had been greatly depleted by the return to the colours of its many reservists, and because of the wide variety of extra duties brought about by the war, which included enforcing the blackout regulations.

These had been required since 20 September 1915, when a lighting order for the city was issued following the air-raids on Sheringham, Yarmouth and King's Lynn. This imposed a complete blackout but exempted churches and railway stations. Trams rattled the streets with a single guttering candle lighting their interiors, the kerbs were sprayed white, it was an offence to light a match in the open and many people wore luminous discs as they stumbled and bumped about the pitch black streets. As there were no air-raid wardens as in the Second World War, it was the task of the specials to patrol the city looking for illegal gleams. During the whole of the war 4,042 people were fined, usually five shillings, for lighting offences. But the inconvenience proved worthwhile for, apart from one nerve-racking overflight by a Zeppelin that missed the city and had to content itself with scattering bombs at random in the surrounding countryside, Norwich remained unscathed.

The social dislocation increasingly caused by the war resulted in comparatively little extra crime. Most of the problems caused by the thousands of soldiers billeted in the city were dealt with by the military police under the control of the provost marshal and soldiers only came under civil jurisdiction if their crimes were not specifically against military discipline. The chief constable was, however, instructed by the council to complain to the military authorities about the reckless and inconsiderate driving of military vehicles.

One result of the military presence that caused most public alarm was the unsettling effect of the troops on the city's young women. An unprecedented outbreak of 'khaki fever', eventually contributing to a 30% national increase in illegitimate births, outraged the proprieties of the staider citizens. In December 1914 the Lord Mayor received a letter signed by sixty-six people that expressed:

> 'deep concern at the conduct of large numbers of our young people. The recent billeting of troops in the city has been accompanied by an outbreak of rowdy and wanton behaviour in the streets, which has shocked public opinion and seriously impaired the city's good name . . . There are standards of decency which no community can allow to be disregarded, without destroying in the minds of the rising generation all reverence for law and order and the elementary principles of civilised life.'[14]

Lack of decorum gave way to open violence on occasions, the magistrates noting that some women had an inclination to obstruct the police with blows and foul language when their soldier companions were arrested for drunkenness. There was a good deal of juvenile crime, caused, in the opinion of the magistrates, by the absence of fathers and elder brothers.

The type of theft and petty crime was similar to before the war but there were some crimes peculiar to the time. A soldier was fined for trying to pass off a franc for a shilling and a confidence trickster preyed on the natural sympathy of the citizens by posing as a bogus Belgian refugee. A whole new range of offences were created by the new licensing regulations which closed the pubs at 9.30 p.m.

Within a few months of the start of the war the pale blue uniform of the convalescent soldier had become almost as equally a familiar sight in the city as khaki. The Red Cross organised a large band of volunteers to run five hospitals in the city: the newly completed Lakenham School on City Road was quickly converted into a hospital, as was Carrow Abbey, the Bishop's Palace, Bracondale Woods and Town Close House. Private individuals offered their houses to the sick although probably in the belief that the war would be over by Christmas. Sunny Hill House at Thorpe, Catton Hall and the Convent of the Little Sisters of the Assumption all took in convalescent troops. But all this medical care was peripheral to the main war hospital which had been set up in the County Asylum at Thorpe in April 1915. Thorpe had two thousand five hundred beds and throughout the course of the war nearly forty-five thousand troops were treated there.[15] The smaller Red Cross hospitals were for the less serious cases and for the sick of locally stationed units. Ambulance trains regularly arrived at Thorpe Station to unload their wounded passengers but if ever the citizens had gathered to cheer them on their way to the hospital and to pelt them with flowers they soon tired of the practice. After four years of war the wounded became commonplace and military funerals were so frequent that complaints were made that men no longer raised their hats when a funeral procession passed by.

Schools were quickly effected by the war, many being used for short periods by the army as emergency billets and canteens. The main hall of the Avenue Schools was given over to the feeding of troops for some months in 1915 to the great dislocation of the school's routine. As the majority of the city's teaching staff were women, enlistment did not create great gaps in the teachers' ranks; only seventeen had joined up after six months and their places were filled with married women on the condition they would be dismissed when, and if, the men returned. The curriculum itself responded to the challenge of wartime circumstances, the older boys at the City of Norwich School being given military training and taken on regular visits to the miniature rifle range while special classes in meatless and economical cooking were arranged for the girls. The Technical Institute – now Norwich Art School – ran courses in commercial and industrial skills for women and girls so that they could take the place of men who had enlisted. The blackout caused great difficulties in continuing evening classes and during the winter months the school day was shortened by as much as two hours. This left the staff with time on their hands and the Education Committee, always loathe to see idle teachers, organised a committee for hospital war work which kept one hundred and thirty of them busy winding bandages, making swabs and knitting pneumonia jackets. 'It will be seen then that the ratepayers have no cause for complaint with regards to the unemployment of the teachers,' the chief education officer noted smugly.[16]

The main worry of the education authorities was the number of boys and girls who left school without completing four years of secondary education because well-paid work was so easy to find. During the war industry gradually attuned itself to war production and jobs were freely available. Pressure of business forced Boulton & Paul, making military aircraft, to expand from their Rose Lane site to Riverside Road. Mann Egerton was making military vehicles, and Laurence Scott electrical equipment for the Navy. The boot and shoe industry was fully stretched making boots for the British army and more unorthodox footware: Howlett and White made Cossack boots for the the Russians, alpine boots for the Italians as well as fur-lined R.A.F. boots.

The local churches organised all kinds of social and philanthropic

69

activities for refugees and soldiers billeted far from home, as well as organising extra services to commend the allied cause. The tone of such services was not quite as jingoistic as we are often led to believe. In January 1915, at a service in the cathedral to mark the day of national intercession the Dean warned the congregation of assuming that God was automatically on their side: 'patriotism is not an exclusively Christian virtue, we have not in this regard excelled Japan, and moreover we have no right in addressing our young men to suggest to them that to fall in battle fighting nobly for their country will straightaway grant to them the death of a saint'.[17] A controversy broke out later as to whether clergy could join the volunteers and a vigorous debate was conducted until firmly closed by the Bishop who ruled, 'there is no place for the clergy in the fighting line at all'.[18]

Entertainment remained determinedly frivolous and only rarely took account of the war. The Prince of Wales Theatre obtained special equipment to show the first films of the war in October 1914, and pictures of the fighting continued to be shown but normally as part of a general programme. While the Hippodrome showed a revue called *The Mystery Gun*, the Theatre De Luxe combined an epic eight reeler *A Study in Scarlet*, with a film of the bombardment of the Turkish forts in the Dardanelles.

Despite the recruiting drives, the flag days for allied nations, the balaclava knitting and bandage winding, not everyone in Norwich was fully committed to the war effort. The Independent Labour Party which was strong in the city maintained its internationalist and pacifist stance continuing to claim that the war was fought only for the benefit of Vickers-Armstrong and Krupp and had no relevance to the real struggle to advance the conditions of working people. In August 1914 they published a resolution that deplored the entry of Britain into the war which drew a public rebuke from Fred Henderson, the leader of the local Labour Party. He pointed out, in case anyone should think that the I.L.P. represented socialist thought generally, that the war was 'just as much a war for the liberation of the German people as for the liberation of civilisation from military truculence. It is the German military bureaucracy we are fighting, not the German people.'[19] His position was further strengthened when the Labour Party joined Asquith's first coalition government in 1915 and one can imagine the embarrassment and outrage when the I.L.P. announced that it was to hold its annual conference in Norwich that Easter.

The Hippodrome had originally been booked for the conference but it was busy with a revue called, appropriately enough, *Get You Away, Boys!* and the Thatched Assembly Rooms was then booked for 4–6 April. When the owner, R. H. Bond, however, learned of who was to occupy his premises he promptly cancelled the booking explaining that 'as a patriotic citizen, it is impossible for me to allow the rooms to be used for such a purpose'.[20] On 1 April the committee of the I.L.P. with Keir Hardie arrived in the city and secretly tried to book other halls but by now all owners were alerted and all efforts were fruitless. For a few days that Easter Norwich was full of most of the anti-war figures in British politics: Ramsay MacDonald, Keir Hardie, Charles Trevelyan and Fenner Brockway, but without anywhere to meet. A letter to the *Eastern Daily Press* suggested that the conference should be held at Mundesley for 'there, possibly, some of our German brothers, if not jeering at drowning women and non-combatant men, might deposit a loving memento in the shape of a 14-inch shell'.[21] Despite the manifest hostility in the city three churches were offered to the conference, the Octagon in Colegate, the Scott Memorial on Thorpe Road and the Queen's Road Primitive Methodist. It took some courage to confront public opinion by offering to take in such political outcasts but the trustees of the Queen's Road church justified their action by stating that they were concerned for the honour of the city and the interests of free speech, which was, after all, what the war was all about. The I.L.P. accepted the offer of the Queen's Road church and the conference with two hundred delegates opened in the schoolroom on 6 April. The delegates were welcomed on behalf of the local party by H. E. Witard who sent a message of gratitude to Karl Liebsknecht, the German socialist, for trying to stem the tide of hatred against the British people. While this and a long message of fraternal greeting from the Social Democratic Party of Russia was being read, the Norwich Volunteer Corps was being inspected on Mousehold Heath by Major-General Daniell, neatly illustrating the polarity of attitudes to the war. The rest of the conference was spent on matters of internal party organisation concluding with a demand to nationalise the railways.[22]

The fundamental disagreements in policy about the war surfaced again in November 1915, when the City Council set up a local tribunal to 'star' men for enlistment. Witard's name was put forward as a member of the tribunal but several members strongly objected, attacking him for refusing to assist in any way with recruiting, to which he replied that his conscience would not allow him to persuade or force others to do something that he would not do himself.

A greater crisis arose in 1917 when the local Labour movement's existing differences were exacerbated to the point of a split. George Roberts, the city's Labour M.P. since 1906, was offered the post of Minister of Labour in the coalition government and this necessitated a by-election for which the writ was moved on 21 August 1917. The local Conservatives and Liberals stated that they would not field a candidate and that Roberts would be unopposed, but then the I.L.P. and Workers and Soldiers Council intimated that they would field a candidate of their own. Roberts' nomination by the Labour Representative Committee was opposed by the powerful Boot and Shoe Operatives who proposed that Witard stand instead. For a tense two days it looked as if the by-election would be fought between two Labour candidates, Witard attacking Roberts on his failure to support the agricultural labourers' demand for a minimum wage of thirty shillings and his hostile attitude to the international socialist conference at Stockholm. However, Roberts could draw on the support of virtually the whole establishment of the city and what was the opposition of the Boot and Shoe Operatives compared to the endorsement of the Lord Mayor, the Chamber of Commerce and the Labour Party's national agent? There was a packed public meeting in the Agricultural Hall, chaired by the Bishop of Thetford, which passed a motion approving, with only a handful of dissenting voices, Roberts' appointment and pledging future support.[23] Faced with this, the opposition faded away and there was no contest.

Food became a problem in 1917 as the German U-boat campaign began to be effective and on 10 August a food control committee was set up with twelve members of the council. These included the Lord Mayor, Alderman Blyth, Sir Eustace Gurney and H. E. Witard who had led a Dear Food and Fuel Campaign in 1915 complaining of the steep rise in the cost of living and demanding that the Government control shipping and fix coal prices. All land that was suitable for growing crops was handed over to the Parks and Gardens Committee which supervised allotments and the cultivation of playing fields. A register was compiled of all available land and those with large gardens could hand over a portion to the committee which would arrange for its cultivation.[24] Official food rationing with coupons did not start until early in 1918.

The early enthusiasm for the war had been eroded to a sort of dogged determination by 1918. The papers were no longer full of letters from the Front and displayed none of the naive enthusiasms of the first year. The news of the Armistice came as something of a surprise, although there had been reports of victories and spectacular advances for the previous three months. The celebrations do not seem to have been quite so exuberant as in London, and apparently were less joyous than those that had greeted the news of the relief of Mafeking, probably because there were so many who had very little to rejoice in. There was a military parade of five thousand men, and two thousand people packed St Peter Mancroft Church for a service of thanksgiving while outside in the Market Place there was a spontaneous unauthorised firework display. This ended with three cheers for the chief constable – rather than the King as might have been expected.

Four years of war had wrought no material damage in Norwich; not a single slate had been displaced by the enemy. But 3,544 men would not return, and the economic, political and social structure of the city had changed in ways unforeseen by those who greeted the outbreak of war so blithely in 1914.

Notes

1. *Eastern Daily Press*, 3 August.
2. Mottram, R. H., *A Window Seat or Life Observed* (London, 1954), p. 216.
3. *Norwich Mercury*, 8 August.
4. Ibid.
5. Ibid.
6. Ibid., 26 August.
7. N.R.O. N/TC/7/20(48).
8. Supplement to *The War Illustrated*, 23 October 1914.
9. *Norwich Mercury*, 31 October.
10. Ibid., 8 August.
11. *Library Committee Report*, 31 March 1917, N.R.O. N/TC/1/58.
12. Leech, H., ed., *Peace Souvenir* (Norwich, 1920), pp. 19–20.
13. Ibid., p. 26.
14. N.R.O. N/TC/7/19.
15. *Peace Souvenir*, p. 41.
16. *Education Committe Report*, 31 March 1916, N.R.O. N/TC/1/58.
17. *Norwich Mercury*, 6 January 1915.
18. Ibid., 6 March 1915.
19. Ibid., 8 August 1914.
20. *Eastern Daily Press*, 1 April 1915.
21. Ibid., 5 April 1915.
22. Ibid., 7 April 1915.
23. *Norwich Mercury*, 22 August 1917.
24. N.R.O. N/TC/1/58.

Land and Labour

by

Nicholas Mansfield

The outbreak of the war did not immediately change the pattern of employment in East Anglia. The harvest of 1914 was brought in before farmworkers of military age trickled through to the recruiting stations. The predominantly arable farmers of East Anglia managed in all but the busiest times of the working year (seedtime and harvest), with their families and older workmen.

The greatest threat to production was the requisitioning of farm horses by government agents. The massive Kitchener armies needed these, not to provide mounts for cavalry, which were irrelevant in the new trench warfare, but to haul the artillery which was to dominate the battlefields, and above all for transport.

By 1915 the national agricultural workforce had dropped by 7% and a poor harvest that year meant that production actually dropped to below pre-war levels. County War Agricultural Committees were appointed to attempt to improve this performance. They tried to increase the available rural workforce. Soldiers stationed in the area were released for harvest and hay-making. This was not always popular in heavily unionised Norfolk as the soldiers were accused of lowering the wages and even strike breaking. This came to a head with a brawl between labourers and soldiers at a recruiting meeting at Great Massingham in 1915.[1] Later, the use of German prisoners of war was similarly disliked.

Women were another source of labour. Many agricultural tasks, particularly in dairying, had once been considered women's work. By late Victorian times, however, there was a move away from the heavy women's field work, such as hoeing, weeding and stonepicking, mostly done on piece rates. This was partly because of legislation against the gang system by which these women were employed, and then largely for reasons of supposed immorality, rather than of improving their conditions. In 1914 some women still worked on the land, but this was mainly seasonal, and apart from harvest these women were thought of as 'rough'.

Now all village women were encouraged by the authorities to leave their cottages for the fields. Even those who had originally campaigned for women to adopt more 'respectable' roles in the home, and for increased wages for their men, took part in this appeal. Thus George Edwards, leader of the farmworkers' union stated early in 1916: 'I am asking you to do a thing which I had hoped you would never have been asked to do again and which, I am thankful to say, the improved conditions of labour have made unnecessary. But the crisis is so great and the danger of losing all that is sacred and good in our national life is so pronounced, that I venture to make this appeal to you to offer your services in cultivating the land in order that as much food can be produced at home as possible. There will be a great deal of work to do in the spring, such as hoeing and weeding, getting the land fit for the turnip crops and many light jobs which hitherto have been done by men.'[2]

The appeal was largely unsuccessful. There was a certain amount of bitterness against Edwards himself, and younger women who wanted to work found better paid jobs making aircraft wings at Savages in King's Lynn or tanks at Burrells of Thetford. Some went further afield and were employed in hospitals or munitions factories. (The accidental death of one young 'munitionette' is recorded on the village war memorial at Longham in Norfolk.) Farmers, too, were deeply suspicious of employing women, and discouraged the first training schemes. From 1915 the authorities attempted to place middle class women in farmwork by recruiting a Forage Corps, which later became the Women's Land Army. However, this was largely a propaganda response to the 1917 U-boat crisis. To judge by national figures, the overall impact of women on the land was small. At a time when women's employment patterns had changed out of all recognition, the number of full time females in agriculture only rose from 80,000 in 1914 to 89,000 in 1918.[3]

Connected with the Women's Land Army, another institution which was to have an enormous impact on women in the countryside appeared in the last year of the war. Women's Institutes originated in Canada, but were encouraged by agricultural authorities as meeting places for sewing, salvage work and jam making!

To compensate for the lack of female labour, East Anglian farmers, through the County Education Committees which they controlled, brought in boy labour. School exemption certificates were issued for farmers who could give work to lads over twelve, and in January 1916 this was extended to girls who could look after younger children to enable their mothers to work. Although there had been a tradition of child labour in peak periods of the farming year, this deprivation of education for a whole generation was surely one of the shameful episodes of the war on the home front. Skilled labour was still short and wages began to rise as the embryonic farmworkers union began to flex its muscles. There was even a threat of a Norfolk strike in February 1915, until a historic meeting between the union and farmers resulted in a negotiated wage rise and the recognition of the union.

Agriculture continued to be unplanned and it was only the success of the German U-boat campaign, coupled with the poor harvest of 1916 that caused the government to act. In January 1917 the Board of Agriculture set up a Food Production Department (F.P.D.). The officials of this organisation were given emergency powers to enforce proper cultivation. They could enter private property, dispossess inefficient farmers of their tenancies, and direct that new land be ploughed up. The F.P.D. organisers were often pioneers of scientific agriculture encouraging new crops such as sugar beet, ironically, as Germany supplied 80% of Britain's pre-war demand for this crop. Tractors began to be imported from America; Randells of North Walsham were the first in the field, supplying the Overtime tractor on licence. F.P.D. men carried cans of petrol around with them to help explain to puzzled farmers how such machines worked. The old County Committees were replaced by smaller seven men County Agricultural Executive Committees which reinforced the F.P.D.'s policies.

At central government level, new commodity commissions (such as the Wheat Executive and the Sugar Commission) were created in 1917, which organised imports, allocating shipping space, and were the major buyers of domestic produce. The Ministry of Munitions became responsible for the development of agricultural machinery, and the supply of fuel oils. It was a major buyer of agricultural products in its own right. In August 1917 it purchased the entire British flax crop to make uniforms, including that of the historic linen trade of the Norfolk/Suffolk border which enjoyed a brief Indian summer due to the war.

Most importantly, in August 1917 the government passed the Corn Production Act. This guaranteed minimum cereal prices for farmers for six years, and established a minimum wage for farmworkers. The minimum wage was set by Agricultural Wages Boards on which employers and unions were represented. This gave the farming industry a boost of confidence which enabled it to make a positive contribution to the war effort. Despite another difficult harvest in 1917, and a food crisis brought on by the success of the German submarines, the introduction of rationing was an indication that the authorities were in control of the situation.

Nevertheless, in November 1918, the government were sufficiently concerned to put the survivors of the 400,000 farmworkers who had enlisted, in the first wave of workers for demobilisation along with miners and transport workers. By and large, farmers had done well out of the war. Prices had risen and had been kept stable by government intervention. Landowners, however, were faced with static rents and high wartime taxation (in 1919 death duties were 40% on estates over £2 million). Land values were still high so in the immediate post-war period there were huge sales. In March 1919, half a million acres were on the market. By 1921 it is estimated that one-quarter of the acreage of England had changed hands since the war's end.[4] In a movement which rivalled the effects of the dissolution of the monasteries or the Civil War, many of the great estates were broken up, and the purchasers were largely the tenants themselves. A new class of owner occupier farmers was created. The large country houses were often retained by the gentry, but the role of the big house started to decline from 1918, and many of them were obliterated in the agricultural crisis of the 1920s and 1930s. The centuries-old triad of squire, tenant farmer and labourer began to decay. From 1919, the Forestry Commission started its work of producing timber to reduce dependence on foreign imports, which was to transform so much of the East Anglian landscape.

Rural society was shaken by the war and the drift of farmworkers from the land accelerated. Bill Curtis of Salhouse: 'There was a lot left after the war. Them what had been soldiers if they could get a job out they did so. Anything that they could get that was better than a farm. A lot of them went into towns like Norwich and them sort of places and got jobs.'[5] Curtis himself, took to lorry driving, abandoning the farming skills by which he had been earning a living. George Ewart Evans, foremost historian of East Anglian rural life concluded: 'the First World War was a definite watershed in the transmission of the traditional lore. For it saw the beginning of mechanisation, and the erosion of the domination of the horse.' Evans makes the interesting point that many farmworkers had learned rough handling habits while working with horses during their war service.[6]

But something else had been changed by the war. The centuries old customs and celebrations of village culture geared to the cyclical nature of the farming year, were gradually replaced by a national popular culture whose agents were the cinema, wireless and daily newspapers. 'Well the Fair stopped. I couldn't tell you what year. Before the First World War. All those old customs dropped off then. I don't think that was picked up then.'[7]

Notes

1. Alun Howkins, *Poor Labouring Men*, London, 1985, p. 118.
2. George Edwards, *From Crowscaring to Westminster*, London, 1922, p. 191.
3. H. W. Wilson and J. A. Hammerton, *The Great War*, Volume 13, p. 34.
4. Arthur Marwick, *The Deluge*, London, 1965, pp. 324–25. Howard Newby, *The Deferential Worker*, London, 1977, p. 63.
5. Interview, 1983. Tape at Norfolk Rural Life Museum, Gressenhall.
6. George Ewart Evans, *Spoken History*, London, 1987, pp. 51 and 52.
7. Ibid., p. 15. Evans was interviewing Priscilla Savage of Blaxhall, Suffolk.

Politics and the Farmworkers Union
by
Nicholas Mansfield

Norfolk was, and is, the bedrock on which the farmworkers union is based. In the 1870s, Joseph Arch organised there, and was returned as M.P. for North West Norfolk during the late Victorian period largely on the farmworkers' vote. However, agricultural depression had destroyed the union until George Edwards, a veteran activist, re-founded it in 1906 as the Eastern Counties Agricultural Labourers and Smallholders Union. Despite heroic work, by the outbreak of the war it was still a regional union of only 350 branches with about 5,000 members. These men were not advanced socialists who opposed the war; 'practically in every village the great bulk of the young men have joined the army. In this way we have for the time being lost nearly all our active and energetic members'.[1]

The shortages of rural labour meant that the union prospered during the war, as more workers, seeing its apparent power to force up wages, joined its ranks. Importantly, it kept in touch with its members in the forces and their subscriptions were regarded as being up to date. Ernie Cornwall of Syderstone comments that 'The thing of it was if you joined the farmworkers you was in the union and (if) you paid your first subscription, when you come out you was a member all that time. You didn't hatta join again'.[2] The deaths of members in the forces were recorded in *The Labourer*, the union's magazine. Later in the war, as the age limit for conscription was extended to 50, many middle aged farmworkers, often of unmilitary character, were called up. A niche was found for them in agricultural companies of the Army Labour Corps, the forerunner of the Pioneer Corps. They were doing the same job as before, but now they were directed to work where they were most needed, usually in another part of the country. Some continued to hold union cards, an illegal act. Evidence of this is in a paid up contribution card for 1918 belonging to Charles Holmes of Crostwick, Norfolk, in the collection of the Norfolk Rural Life Museum at Gressenhall. Holmes served in Yorkshire and settled there, marrying a local woman. The Corn Production Act of 1917, which established a minimum wage and achieved official recognition of the union, gave a further boost to recruitment in East Anglia. By the end of the war, over 1,500 branches were claimed.

The outlook of many farmworkers in the army was changed by mixing with men from other parts of the country. George Howell of Walsingham served in the 10th Essex Regiment with London stevedores: 'It was an education to me which I shouldn't have got. It learnt me a lot which I shouldn't have got otherwise'.[3] After years of suffering in France, the Norfolk farmworkers returned determined that something must change. The union was the first recipient of this determination, and the numbers shot up nationally to 127,000 by the end of 1919. In Norfolk, membership increased from 6,500 to 21,000.[4] One organisation which radicalised the farmworkers was the National Federation of Discharged Sailors and Soldiers formed in 1917. It had a left wing programme advocating full employment, unemployment benefit of £2 a week, and nationalisation of land and industry. It was especially critical of the 'Comrades of the Great War', an ex-service organisation founded by Conservatives. Indeed, the Federation debarred officers from membership unless they had risen from the ranks. In the immediate post war period, the Federation was active in Norfolk and in 1919, disrupted meetings of the Comrades in Norwich, King's Lynn and East Dereham. In August 1920, the Federation joined with the Comrades and other ex-service organisations to form the British Legion, but its activists found a new role in the Labour Party.

Socialism was weak in East Anglia before the war. There were some exceptions to this, Norwich had one Independent Labour M.P. from 1906 and Ipswich had an active socialist party. At Burston, near Diss, in 1914, schoolchildren supported by their parents, came out on strike when their two socialist schoolteachers were unjustly dismissed. The Labour movement rallied round to raise funds to open an alternative school in 1917 which offered non-sectarian education. The Burston Strike School remained open for 25 years and still stands, the scene of an annual rally by the farmworkers union. It is, however, worth pointing out that Tom Higdon, one of the schoolteachers, presided at army recruiting meetings until the introduction of conscription. The farmworkers had traditionally supported the Liberals, but now the Liberals were demoralised by the authoritarian climate forced by the war, and split by the decision of their leader, Lloyd George, to persist with a National Government.

Lloyd George won the 'Khaki' election in December 1918, but a new force was active in the shape of the Labour Party. The farmworkers union affiliated to it, and union activists like George Edwards left the Liberals and joined Labour. They were even followed by some of the great Liberal landowners like the Kimberleys and the Buxtons. Noel Buxton, who had been radical Liberal M.P. for North Norfolk before joining Labour, became Minister of Agriculture in the Labour governments of 1924 and 1929. Although it narrowly failed to win any Parliamentary seats in 1918, Labour made inroads into local government, and in 1920 succeeded in electing George Edwards as M.P. for South Norfolk in a by-election. Its rural policy of smallholdings, allotments, the abolition of tied cottages and government support for agriculture, seized the imagination of a generation of young men who had been through the war.

Bill Curtis of Salhouse, aged 22, was one of these: 'They used to have these demonstrations everywhere after that for a few years. Just getting people to join and telling the people the facts of life and all this, that and the other. Tell the truth of how men worked and how they'd been treated. You'd march with a band from one end of Wroxham right down to the other end, over the bridge . . . I used to go round on an old bike weekends, Saturdays and Sundays, having meetings in different villages.'[5] Tom Barker of Erpingham describes the scene after the election of Noel Buxton in 1924: 'They never really come out into the open in Gresham until Lord Noel Buxton (who was Noel Buxton then), won the seat for Labour. And then they came out with the red flag which the women had made and they marched up and down from one end of Gresham to the other. When Buxton got into Parliament I was at school. I remember them coming past the school kicking up a row and such like. They come right out into the open and quite a number on 'em got the sack anyway. He (their employer) had to take 'em back. Labour had got in.'[6]

Labour soon controlled certain rural districts where its policies, particularly on public health and the building of council houses were implemented. Smallholding settlements, with priority for ex-servicemen, were formed by County Councils with all-party support. But these had a poor level of capital investment, and most went under during the agricultural depression. The farmworkers' block vote was in evidence for a generation and more, culminating in the 1945 General Election when Norfolk returned seven Labour M.P.s. Then, even Cambridgeshire, traditional provider of blacklegs in farming disputes, returned Alf Stubbs, local farmworker union leader, for Labour, for the first and only time. Such rural seats as South West Norfolk and North Norfolk remained Labour until 1964 and 1970.

In June 1921, the Corn Production Act was repealed, leaving prices and wages once more to the vagaries of the market place. Farm prices fell sharply and farmers dismissed their workers and tried to make ends meet using family labour, or machinery, reducing standards and grassing over previously arable land. The farmworkers union could do little about falling wages and increasing unemployment, causing great bitterness, particularly among the ex-servicemen. Matters came to a head in March 1923, when Norfolk farmworkers went on strike to resist a wage cut to below 25 shillings a week. As the farmers recruited agricultural students to help them drill the vital corn seed, the strike became bitter. In the words of George Edwards: 'We have not seen the worst of the struggle yet . . .

81

Norfolk sent a large proportion of men to the services. Now they are back and they find themselves cruelly deceived . . . these men have the war spirit, and however much I regret this spirit I am sure that it is going to show itself if this dispute continues another ten days.'[7]

The younger men organised marching pickets to stop 'blacklegs' working. Almost all of them '. . . were ex-soldiers. The military precision of the route marches, the use of bugles, frequent mention of medal ribbons and khaki greatcoats in the press, all point to this. So does the fact that meetings and marches began and ended not just on village greens but specifically at war memorials'.[8] Men who had survived the Somme were not afraid of young farmers' sons who were taking their work. In a violent scene at Rougham a blackleg was assaulted and asked; 'Where were you in 1914? . . . We have been through five years of war. You make your pile in the war and we are going to have it now'. In another incident a striker was reported as saying: 'This is a revolution; we fought for the land and we are going to have it'.[9]

These 'wild gangs', as one veteran described them, marched long distances to areas where they would not be identified. There was considerable sympathy from local policemen, often ex-soldiers themselves, causing the authorities to bring in policemen from Yorkshire, London and Hertfordshire. Ernie Cornwall: 'Well there was one place where our policeman he come past us wheeling his bike and they (the strikers) see these here (the blacklegs) and he say to the men he say "Stop somewhere out of the way then you can go after them".'[10] According to another witness: 'The policemen would turn their backs when we went over the hedge'.[11]

Bill Curtis was part of a 'wild gang': 'Blokes went round having a look round to see who was out and who wasn't . . . There was some blokes working in the field and they took the horses off and sent the horses home and took 'em onto the road . . . They didn't do much to 'em. Daren't because the police was so sharp on 'em see? . . . I was supposed to be at Smallburgh at the time, but the (defence) lawyer said I wasn't there. I was there but that don't matter, they got evidence to say I wasn't there.'[12]

Not all were as lucky as Curtis and many men were fined or imprisoned. Public opinion, already behind the strikers, was increased after it was reported that a striker sentenced at Walsingham courthouse wore his Mons Star in court. After three weeks, with both sides exhausted by the struggle, a compromise was negotiated by Ramsay MacDonald, the Labour leader. The men returned to work at the old rate of 25 shillings a week. The downward drift of wage cuts had been stopped, but agriculture itself continued to be depressed, and many of the ex-soldiers found other work, sometimes after long periods of unemployment. The land fit for heroes was not to materialise under the wide East Anglian skies.

Notes

1. Howard Newby, *The Deferential Worker*, London, 1977, p. 216. Quoting Annual Union Report 1914.
2. Interview, 1983. Tape at Norfolk Rural Life Museum.
3. Ibid.
4. Alun Howkins, *Poor Labouring Men*, London, 1985, p. 122.
5. Interview, 1983. Tape at Norfolk Rural Life Museum.
6. Ibid.
7. Quoted in Reg Groves, *Sharpen the Sickle*, London, 1949, p. 186.
8. Alun Howkins, op. cit., p. 167
9. Ibid., p. 168.
10. Interview, 1983. Tape at Norfolk Rural Life Museum.
11. Interview with Edgar Wicks of East Rudham, Tape,1982.
12. Interview, 1983. Tape at Norfolk Rural Life Museum.

For Valour. Victoria Cross awards to men from Norfolk and Suffolk, 1914–18

by
Philip Bujak

From its inception in 1857 the Victoria Cross has taken precedence over all other British Orders and medals. The mystique surrounding those who have gained this award is understandable in that it is so difficult to quantify what it takes to win the Victoria Cross. The award is not restricted to any particular social class or rank and there does not seem to be any discernible pattern of lifestyle that would help us to understand more about the nature of courage. It is certainly true to say that those men from Norfolk and Suffolk who gained the award during the Great War were from the widest possible parts of county society. What then inspired these men to their actions? Was it a form of battle madness, extreme anger or perhaps just plain fear, something, in other words, common to us all? Were these men leaders in other walks of life before service with the colours or dragged from obscurity by the award of a bronze medal with the Crimean ribbon?

Between 1856 and 1914, a total of 522 Victoria Crosses had been awarded. However in the years 1914–18 633 were won. Of these 415 were to the British Army (124 awarded posthumously), 51 to members of the navy and marines, 9 to the R.F.C. and R.A.F. and 158 to Dominion or Indian Army personnel. Of all these, a total of 187 were posthumous.[1] More awards were made in this single period than at any other time both before or since.

Norfolk and Suffolk produced their share of those who gained the highest award 'for valour'. Included in this series of mini-biographies are both those of men who were born in the two counties and those who were serving in the county regiments. The acts were performed by men from the various social divisions of the regions, who were farmers, farmworkers or sons of craftsmen. Of them all perhaps C.S.M. Daniels conforms to the classic picture of a hero and the story of Lt.Col. Jack Kelly has the makings of the most interesting full biography. The following short biographies of five Suffolk and five Norfolk men illustrate some of the acts of outstanding bravery which shone out among those four years of chaos and suffering.

Gordon Murial Flowerdew was born at Billingford, near Scole, 2 January 1885. He was baptised at St Leonard's Church, Billingford on 1 March 1885. Gordon Flowerdew came from a large family. His parents, A. J. Bloomfield Flowerdew and Hannah Flowerdew had fifteen children, ten boys and five girls, whose names are all recorded in the parish register. Mr Arthur Flowerdew was a farmer, one of whose ancestors had been a steward to the Duke of Norfolk in 1557, and the family lived at Billingford Hall near Diss. All ten sons attended Framlingham College in Suffolk.[2]

Completing his education between 1894 and 1899 Gordon Flowerdew worked on the family farm as a young man. His younger sister, Mrs Lorna Tillot, explained in 1970 that Gordon was always 'fidgetty and full of go'[3] and emigrated to Canada in 1903. At the start of the war he joined Lord Strathcona's Horse, as did his brother Eric who was only sixteen at the time. On 30 March 1918 Lieutenant Flowerdew was in the line trying to stem the desperate German advance in the Bois de Moreuil. The official war history notes that 'which ever brigade arrived first should make straight for the high ground north-west of the wood'. The Canadian Cavalry Brigade were already saddled up, had the shorter distance to go and moved quickly. It was spurred on by alarming news imparted to Brigadier General Seely at the cross roads near Castel by a French General who said the Germans were advancing in overwhelming force and that he had sent orders for his troops to fall back across the Avre: indeed they had already done so, for the Germans had moved to the attack of the allied south of the Somme at 8 a.m.

By 9.30 a.m., as the Canadians approached the wood, there was considerable fire from the northern face; but on the western side from which the Germans could see the smoke of Amiens – the slope permitted a defiled advance up to about two hundred yards from the edge. The Royal Canadian Dragoons were sent mounted against the south-west and north-west corners, while Lord Strathcona's Horse, supported by four machine guns placed in the unoccupied detached portion of the wood, attacked with two squadrons dismounted against the north face and with one mounted against the north-east corner. The squadron charged through a line of guns, and some of the survivors entered the wood from the east. It was this squadron which was commanded by Lt. Flowerdew. He charged between two lines of Germans, each sixty strong, and put a machine-gun post out of action. The Official History continues '. . . the other squadrons had succeeded in breaking in and fierce hand to hand fighting ensued. The Germans stood well, even advanced with the bayonet; but with British airmen assisting the attack they were gradually forced to give ground and by 11.00 a.m. the whole of the northern part of the woods was in Canadian hands.' It has been claimed that Lt.

Flowerdew's action played a significant part in stopping the German advance here and therefore in France as a whole. However Lt. Flowerdew did not escape unscathed from this encounter and he was taken to Namps au Val south-west of Amiens where there was probably a military hospital. It was here that he died of his wounds the next day. Recommended for the award of the Victoria Cross by Brigadier John Seely (later Lord Mottistone), he is named on the war memorial in the local church and is buried in the British cemetery at Namps au Val, Plot 1, Row H, Grave No. 1. There are several Flowerdew memorials in Billingford Church. A. J. Munnings depicted his charge and the original painting is located in the Canadian Houses of Parliament in Ottawa.

Harry Cator was born on 24 January 1894 at Drayton in Norfolk, four miles north-west of Norwich. Later in life he was to be called one of the finest fighting soldiers of the First World War.

His father had been a railway worker and Harry had been educated in Drayton. Described as resourceful, cheerful, hard working and courageous he like thousands of others joined the army when war broke out in 1914.

He served with the East Surrey Regiment in France throughout the war. Fighting and surviving the early battles in Flanders, earned him the 1914–15 Star and he showed his courageous nature when he was awarded the Military Medal in August 1916 being recommended for the award by Major General Scott of 12 Division.

His brother remembered him as '. . . an ordinary sort of chap, but one who would always stand his ground. He was the sort of person who, if there was a job that had to be done, would get on and do it.'[4] On 9 April 1917 he found himself with his battalion, the 7th East Surreys, facing the Hindenburg line near Arras. It was here that he was to win the medal for gallantry that would help make him one of the most decorated Norfolk men in either of the two world wars.

The 7th battalion went over the top at 5.30 a.m. and advanced with considerable success for about an hour when they came under heavy machine gun fire and suffered many casualties. It was at this point, as the advance through the German trenches faltered, that Sergeant Cator took control as his official citation recalls:

'In full view of the enemy and under heavy fire Sergeant Cator with one man advanced across the open to attack the hostile machine gun. The man accompanying him was killed after going a short distance, but Sergeant Cator continued on, and picking up a Lewis gun and some ammunition drums on the way, succeeded in reaching the northern end of the hostile trench.

'Meanwhile, one of our bombing parties was seen to be held up by a machine gun. Sergeant Cator took up a position from which he sighted this gun and killed the entire team and the officer, whose papers he brought in.

Enrolling of women into the Land Army, West Barsham, 1917
(Norfolk Museum Service)

Women's Land Army Young woman in uniform feeding cattle, 1915/16
(Norfolk Museum Service)

Signalwoman, Great Eastern Railway, *c* 1917, Burnham Market
(Norfolk Museum Service)

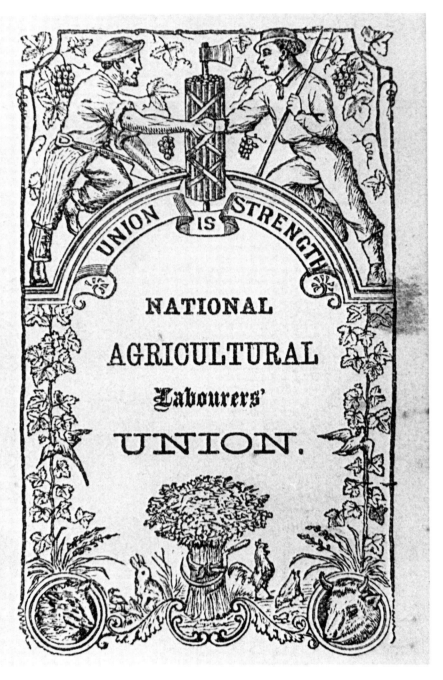

National Agricultural Labourer's Union contribution card
(Norfolk Museum Service)

Sgt. Harry Cator

Lt. Col. John Sherwood-Kelly

Sgt. Claude Castleton

Cpl. Sidney Day

C.S.M. Harry Daniels

Lt. Gordon Flowerdew

Sgt. Arthur Saunders

Lance Cpl. Arthur Cross

Drummer Spencer Bent

Lance Cpl. Ernest Seaman

The Market Place, Lavenham, with 16th Century Guildhall (Kevin Allen)

72 Water Street, Lavenham (Pte. William Smith)

9 Bolton Street, Lavenham, now High Hall (Pte. Harold Lester)

82 Church Street, Lavenham (Pte. Frederick T. Smith)

Church of St Peter and St Paul, Lavenham

War Memorial Book, Lavenham Church

War Memorial, Lavenham Church

Memorial to Sec. Lt. O. W. Wolton, Lavenham Churchyard

'He continued to hold that end of the trench with the Lewis gun with such effect that the bombing squad was enabled to work along, the result being one hundred prisoners and five machine guns were captured.' This citation was published in the *London Gazette* on 8 June 1917.

Although under continuous fire for much of his action Harry Cator, unlike his companion, managed to survive even though his tunic was riddled with bullets. But only three days later his luck ran out when a shell blast shattered his jaw.

It was while he was recovering in a military hospital in Bristol that he learned that he had been awarded the Victoria Cross.

His reaction to the publicity surrounding the Victoria Cross was predictably calm. Although his post war career was unspectacular he came through the years of the depression and had a variety of jobs, initially however being forced to draw dole money. He worked for the Post Office and the National Assistance Board and during the Second World War was given a commission, having rejected one while in the army, and was commandant at a P.O.W. camp near Cranwich.

Like many others he found that not only were there few 'homes fit for heroes' but precious few jobs for them either. Harry Cator died in 1966 at the age of seventy-two and was buried in a simple ceremony in Sprowston churchyard, proud of his medals for gallantry, but never having exploited the glamour that went with them.

Corporal Sidney James Day was the second of the two men from the Norwich area to be awarded the Victoria Cross. A native of Norwich, Sidney Day was educated at St Mark's School, Lakenham, the parish to which he returned after the Great War.

It was while serving with the Suffolk Regiment that Corporal Day won his award. On 24 August 1917 the 11th Suffolks were in the line at Priel Wood – Malakhoff Farm, – Hargicourt:

The citation read:

'For most conspicuous bravery. Cpl. Day was in command of a bombing section detailed to clear a maze of trenches still held by the enemy. This he did, killing two machine gunners and taking four prisoners. On reaching a point where the trench had been levelled he went alone and bombed his way through to the left in order to gain touch with the neighbouring troops. Immediately on his return to his section a stick-bomb fell into the trench occupied by two officers (one badly wounded) and three other ranks. Cpl. Day seized the bomb and threw it over the trench, where it immediately exploded. This prompt action saved the lives of those in the trench. He afterwards completed the clearing of the trench and established himself in an advanced position, remaining for sixty-six hours at his post, which came under intense hostile shell and rifle grenade fire.

Throughout the entire operation his conduct was an inspiration to us all.'[5]

Later he fell into enemy hands but contrary to popular conceptions about the Germans he felt no resentment towards the German soldier. They also had a great respect for the Victoria Cross as he explained after the war; 'The first man to shake hands and congratulate me on receiving the honour was a German soldier, while I was a prisoner in Germany.'

With demobilisation Cpl. Day was placed on the Government Training Scheme for ex-servicemen and eventually found employment with the Norwich Electricity Department then located in Duke Street.

In 1929, commenting on the Lord Mayor's speech on employment for ex-servicemen, Cpl. Day echoed what was patently obvious yet often ignored when he said; 'I don't think employers in general have had that consideration for ex-servicemen that they ought. They have shown too great a tendency to take for granted all that these men went through in the war. They don't seem to realise what the men really endured.'[6]

One of the first Suffolk men to receive the award of the Victoria Cross was **Spencer John Bent** who was born at the Pickerel Inn in Stowupland Street, Stowmarket in 1891.

His early days were spent in the rural surroundings of the valley of the River Gipping and nearby Spikes Farm. This picturesque landscape in summer even today sparks the imagination into visions of a former time of turn-of-the-century rural England.

In 1905, like so many others in early Edwardian England, Joe Bent, as he was later to be known, took the King's Shilling and enlisted in the 1st Battalion of the East Lancashire Regiment at the age of fourteen. He served for a period as a drummer and then in 1914, as part of the British Expeditionary Force his battalion formed part of the reserve at the first battle of Mons. The massive weight of the German attack in its initial stages built up momentum and the East Lancashires were forced to retire at Cambrai and later played their part in halting the Germans on the Marne.

By the autumn therefore Joe Bent had already seen heavy fighting and could count himself among the lucky ones when his unit was moved forward into the Armentières–Ypres front. An article written in 1985 recounted the tale that a false order to retire was causing men to fall back. Joe remembered a French trumpet he had seen and returning to his trench where his platoon sergeant ordered him to stand fast as no retirement order had been issued.

Early next morning the expected German attack materialised after a preliminary bombardment and at an approximate range of 400 yards the Lancashires opened fire. During this action, when all the officers had either been killed or wounded Joe Bent took charge and held their position against heavy enemy fire. The following day he went on to rescue a Private McNulty who had been wounded outside the relative protection of their trench. Under heavy fire Bent retrieved him by placing his legs under

Pte. McNulty's shoulders and, using his elbows, hauled him back into the trench.

Soon after this series of events Joe Bent was badly wounded in his right leg and eventually found himself convalescing back in his native Suffolk. The *London Gazette* announced some weeks later that Drummer Bent had been awarded the Victoria Cross in recognition of his heroic action. In January 1915 he received his award at Buckingham Palace from King George V. Legend has it that after leaving the palace he removed the medal from his chest to avoid being recognised. Perhaps it was true that he was reluctant to be in the public glare. Certainly every award of the Victoria Cross was accompanied by a wave of articles, photographs and drawings illustrating the heroic deed or deeds which were published in newspapers and periodicals during the longer than expected duration of the war.

S. J. Bent served in the British Army for 21 years and was a member of the Old Contemptibles Association. He died on 3 May 1977 at the age of 86.

In July 1985 his medal returned to London, this time to be auctioned at Christie's, where it fetched £12,000.[7]

The Somme, inevitably, was the scene of some of the most courageous acts of heroism. It was here in Picardy that **Claud Charles Castleton** was to perform perhaps one of the most prodigious acts of heroism in the whole of the Great War.

He was born on 12 April 1893 and was educated at the Morton Road School, Lowestoft. Clearly intelligent he won a scholarship to the town's grammar school and performed well in most subjects, finding geography his favourite subject. It is in this that perhaps we find a clue to his clear love for travel. Having spent many of his holidays exploring the waterways of the Norfolk Broads and working in his first job as a student teacher Claud Castleton gave in to his design for travel. In 1912 he sailed for Australia and from Melbourne he went on to work his way eventually to Port Moresby in New Guinea where he went to prospect for gold. His plans to see India and Africa would however never be realised as news of war in Europe reached him. He enlisted in the Australian Imperial Force on 10 March 1915. Seeing action with the ANZACS both in Egypt and Gallipoli he found himself with three Australian battalions on the slopes of Pozières in Picardy, France on the night of 28–29 July 1916.

At the age of twenty-three Sergeant Castleton had been transferred to the 5th Machine Gun Company a few months earlier and watched his comrades of his former 18th battalion move forward prior to the attack at 12.15 a.m. on 29 July. His task was to hold his position against a possible counter attack. The mood of the troops was already pessimistic. The Somme advances had been continuing unabated for weeks, despite frightening casualties. As if to confirm their premonitions the Germans struck first some thirty-five minutes before the ANZACS attack. German shells poured down on the assembly areas and machine-guns cut down hundreds moving towards the start lines, only three hundred yards from the German trenches. The familiar scene of the lunar-like landscape was soon littered with dead and wounded Australians. To venture out from cover was suicidal yet Sergeant Castleton, well aware of his own chances of survival went out and returned with a wounded man over his back. Once again he turned and minutes later, with the physical and mental strain showing, he brought back another infantryman. These deeds alone under intense enemy fire would surely have been rewarded with a decoration of the highest order yet for a third time Sergeant Castleton went out to rescue another. This time his luck and daring did not hold out. Nearly back to safety he was fatally wounded. The first aid team too went out into no-man's-land to drag his body back. The German fire continued until 3 a.m. but no ground had been lost, or gained.

Sergeant C. C. Castleton, the son of a Lowestoft builder was recommended for the Victoria Cross which was approved posthumously on 26 September 1916, when the Somme battles were still being fought.

His sacrifice saved two men from agonising deaths untended and his reputation among his colleagues is testified by an extract of a letter written to his parents:

'. . . we looked to Claud as our leader . . . up to the time of his death we were ready to follow him anywhere.'

The location of this particular medal is still a mystery at the time of writing. Formerly in the hands of Sergeant Castleton's niece it has since disappeared.[8]

The first Suffolk born man serving in the county regiment to win the Victoria Cross was **Sergeant Arthur Frederick Saunders** of the 9th (Service) Battalion, Suffolk Regiment.

During the fighting at Loos 25–26 September 1915, Sergeant Saunders was awarded the V.C. in the words of the *London Gazette*;

'For most conspicuous bravery. When his officer had been wounded in the attack he took charge of two machine guns and a few men and, although severely wounded in the thigh, closely followed the last four charges of another battalion and rendered every possible support. Later when the remains of the battalion which he had been supporting had been forced to retire, he continued to give clear orders, and by his continuous firing did his best to cover the regiment.'[9]

At Scole, on the Norfolk/Suffolk border, there is a memorial to **L/Cpl. Ernest Seaman**. In writing about him in a short article in 1978, Canon W. M. Lummis said 'He was a most unlikely person to have been awarded the highest decoration for valour.'[10]

He had been turned down for active service in December 1915 for medical reasons and had served in the canteens behind the lines of the

Expeditionary Force at Etaples. As casualty figures reached alarming proportions he found himself serving in the front line with the Inniskilling Fusiliers.

The citation published in the *London Gazette* stated:

'For most conspicuous bravery and devotion to duty, 29 September 1918, near Terhand, Belgium. When the right flank of his company was held up by a nest of enemy machine guns he, with great courage and initiative, rushed forward under heavy fire with his Lewis gun and engaged the position single-handed, capturing two machine guns and twelve prisoners and killing one officer and two men. Later in the day he again rushed another enemy machine gun position, capturing the gun under heavy fire. He was killed immediately after.

'His courage and dash were beyond all praise, and it was entirely due to the very gallant conduct of L/Cpl. Seaman that his company was enabled to push forward to its objective and capture many prisoners.'

His company commander said of him later that:

'He was one of the best soldiers whom I had ever met, an excellent soldier in every sense of the word, and very keen on his duties. He always volunteered to help in any extra work that had to be done, no matter how dangerous or difficult, and for his constant devotion to duty and gallantry in voluntarily attending his wounded under heavy fire, I recommend his being awarded the Military Medal.' High praise indeed but one wonders what he would have had to have done to be recommended for the ultimate award for devotion to duty?

In any event in the fighting at Ypres and Passchendaele he earned a posthumous V.C. for two specific acts of gallantry.

One Norfolk recipient of the Victoria Cross who survived the Great War was **Arthur Henry Cross**.

Born at Shipdham on 13 December 1884 his father was Mr William Cross, a wheelwright and carpenter of Market Street, Shipdham between Dereham and Watton. His mother, Emma, also had three daughters one of whom had died in infancy at the age of eleven months. As a boy Arthur Cross attended the Congregational Church at Shipdham and received a bible when he left dated 21 March 1898.

After working with the local butcher for a while at the age of 18 he left for London where he worked first for the Great Eastern Railway and later at the Royal Dockyard, Woolwich. Clearly intent on making London his home, he married Frances a young lady from Camberwell.

On 30 May 1916 Arthur Cross enlisted under the Derby scheme at Flodden Road, Camberwell in the 21st Battalion, The London Regiment (1st Surrey Rifles) and was posted to France as part of 142 Brigade, 47th Division. Later he joined 40th Battalion Machine Gun Corps (the 'Suicide Club' as these units were often known) which was part of 121 Brigade.

However it was not until March and April 1918 that his bravery was recognised first with the Victoria Cross and later with the Military Medal.

His Victoria Cross was awarded for gallantry at Ervilliers on the Somme on 25 March 1918. The *London Gazette* announced in June of that year:

'No. 62995, Arthur Henry Cross, L/Cpl. 40th Bn. Machine Gun Corps. For most conspicuous bravery and initiative. Cross volunteered to make a reconnaissance of the position of two machine guns which had been captured by the enemy. He advanced single handed to the enemy trench, and with his revolver forced seven of the enemy to surrender and carry the machine guns with their tripods and ammunition to our lines. He then handed over his prisoners, collected teams for his guns, which he brought into action with extreme dash and skill, annihilating a very heavy attack by the enemy. It is impossible to speak too highly of the extreme gallantry, initiative and dash displayed by this N.C.O. who showed throughout four days of operations supreme devotion to duty.'[11]

At Bullecourt on 18 May 1918, Sergeant Cross was also awarded the Military Medal for bravery.

The national impact of certain V.C. winners is well illustrated by the award to Sgt. Cross. He received his V.C. from King George V on 4 September 1918 together with a reception in Southwark led by the Mayor of the borough. This event was illustrated in the *Times History of the War* which also showed his family and new born son nicknamed the 'Little V.C.' Eleven days later he was back in Shipdham as a report in the *Eastern Daily Press* (17.9.18) shows him receiving commendations from his old schoolmasters and friends and a gold watch from the village as recognition of his courage.

Public admiration on a still larger scale was shown for **Company-Sergeant Major Harry Daniels** in 1915 by thousands of the citizens of Norwich.

The son of a Norwich baker C.S.M. Daniels was awarded the Victoria Cross while serving with 2nd Battalion The Rifle Brigade (the Prince Consort's Own) at Neuve Chapelle in March 1915.

It was the third day of the ill-fated British offensive near the northern French village and progress had been agonisingly slow and costly. The remnants of C and D companies of the 2nd Rifle Brigade lay a mere 400 yards from the German front lines. Opportunities to attack while the Germans were still disorganised had been thwarted by a series of cancellation orders and now at 4.45 p.m. on 15 March the order came to attack.

Now that all hope of a successful assault had been lost it was to be 'pressed home regardless of loss' in the words of their HQ message.

Facing the men of D company was not only an enemy position equipped with machine guns but also open ground covered with uncut wire. C.S.M. Daniels was ordered by the company commander to detail a party to cut a channel through the wire prior to the attack. Instead he turned to his close friend Cpl. Tom Noble and said 'Come on Tom, get some nippers.' The two men jumped out from their trench straight into enemy fire. They survived their dash and began frantically cutting the wire which ranged from a few inches to several feet in height. Harry Daniels was shot clean through his left thigh but carried on working at the wire lying on his back. Soon after Cpl. Noble was also hit this time mortally in the chest. Cpl. Noble carried on cutting the wire. 'Again and again he did this until he grew so feeble that at last he sank back . . . insensible and soon died,' Daniels recalled later. C.S.M. Daniels remained in no-man's-land for four hours when eventually he crawled back to his own lines. Six weeks later while recovering from his wounds in hospital he learnt he had been awarded the Victoria Cross together with his friend Tom Noble.

By June he was back in Norwich, a city he had not seen for eleven years, for a series of events marking his award. For some the Victoria Cross had come posthumously with honours paid after death while for others it was a great distinction immortalised in drawings and reports in the national press. Willingly or not, to have been awarded the nation's highest honour meant fame though seldom fortune. In C.S.M. Daniels' case it meant both. Staying with relatives at 48 Sussex Street, Norwich, he and his wife were entertained to a string of celebratory occasions culminating in a presentation, prior to his departure for regular duty once more, at the Soldiers' and Sailors' Institute. From one of the upper windows of the Institute the *Eastern Daily Press* described the 'warrior' as addressing the crowd in homely phrases about the tough fight Britain had on her hands. He went on to say that it was the bounden duty of every young fellow who was able to do so to get into khaki and go out and help the British soldiers engaged in this struggle. Other speeches followed as well as the presentation of a 'purse' containing £20 from the Sheriff Mr Frances Horner. 'We are all proud that a Norwich man' said the Sheriff, 'has obtained the highest honour that his Majesty the King can confer on a soldier, and in doing so he has added another name to the roll of illustrious citizens who have rendered conspicuous and distinguished service to their country'. In response C.S.M. Daniels went on to thank all those who had helped to arrange his visit but in reference to his medal said:

'As for the V.C., it does not appeal to me as high act of gallantry, although the civilian population think it does. A soldier looks upon this thing as just his duty.' The wave of applause that greeted this remark concluded his visit to Norwich. After a procession to Thorpe Station passing cheering crowds via Queen Street, Bank Plain and Prince of Wales Road C.S.M. Daniels left by the 6.00 p.m. train for London to rejoin his regiment.[12]

Placed in context this reaction to C.S.M. Daniels is hardly surprising. By this stage few awards had been made while the degeneration of the conflict on the western front to its almost inhuman and featureless nature was still continuing. The British patriotic spirit was resilient and ceremonial such as these events in Norwich served to inject the domestic population with even greater zeal for the fight. The modesty shown by C.S.M. Daniels towards his Victoria Cross was admirable although his picture of the common soldiers view of 'duty' would have, in all likelihood, found few advocates as the war progressed from mid 1916.

Yet Harry Daniels was perhaps one of the best examples of late Victorian and Edwardian ideals. Serving with the colours for nine years in India and gaining a fine array of sporting trophies, mostly for boxing, his rapid rise through the ranks was crowned with a commission in 1915. He was a front line soldier of the first order, 'A born leader, gay, light-hearted and very brave, he terrified me out of my life!' commented one of his former officers.

Peacetime saw Harry Daniels take a post as chief recruiting officer in the north-west, having first been part of the 1920 British Olympic team at Antwerp as a boxer, and later assistant provost-marshall at Aldershot. He finally left the army in 1942.

His appointment to the rank of Honorary Lt. Colonel helped him to undertake a series of managerial posts from a Suffolk hotel to the Odeon Cinema in Leeds. By the mid 1950s he was a popular resident manager of the Leeds Grand Theatre and Opera House which he naturally ran efficiently and with colourful charm. He was about to attend the Queen's coronation when he suffered a heart attack. Norwich's first winner of the Victoria Cross died a few months later on the evening of his 69th birthday.

Another heroic figure associated with Norfolk was **Lt.Col. Jack Sherwood-Kelly, V.C., D.S.O., C.M.G.**, the most decorated man in the history of the Norfolk Regiment. Yet, unlike Harry Daniels, his Victoria Cross did not guarantee him an immortality above reproach in the post-war period. Far from it, his revered military record was to end in court martial, premature retirement and an early death in 1931.

He had already seen action in Matabeleland and Somaliland and according to an account published in the *Daily Express* after 1918, had been so keen to get to the front in 1914 he had enlisted as a private under an assumed name. Having been promoted in the field during the second battle of Ypres he then saw service at Gallipoli in 1915 before returning to the western front.

At Marcoing during the battle of Cambrai, 20–21 November 1917, Major John Sherwood-Kelly, of the Norfolks, was commanding a battalion of the Royal Inniskilling Fusiliers attempting to cross a canal. The neighbouring unit, detailed to give covering fire, was held up by the enemy. At once Sherwood-Kelly ordered covering fire and led the leading

94

company across the canal and then advanced to the high ground held by the enemy. The rest of his battalion on the left flank also began to falter as they encountered wire entanglements. Again Sherwood-Kelly acted swiftly to try to maintain the momentum of the attack. He took a Lewis gun team through the wire and covered the advance of the left flank which thus allowed the position to be captured.

By the end of the action Sherwood-Kelly had captured five machine guns, forty-six prisoners and killed a large number of the enemy. For this action acting Lt.Colonel John Sherwood-Kelly, C.M.G., D.S.O., was awarded the Victoria Cross announced in the *London Gazette* 11 January 1918. By the end of the war Sherwood-Kelly had been wounded five times in action and mentioned in despatches on seven occasions.

The hero of Cambrai had volunteered for the hastily organised Russian Relief Force in May 1919. The aim of the expedition was to support the hard pressed British contingent already fighting the Bolsheviks in north Russia and to help facilitate their evacuation.

As the Commanding Officer of a battalion he did not fit the expected role of leading from the rear. Instead he lived up to his reputation as fearless fighter even being involved in leading small patrols and close combat himself.

However, a brilliant soldier he might have been but the role of the British army in Russia was to him ambiguous. The initial aim had been to keep Russia in the war against Germany and Austro-Hungary thus maintaining the war on two fronts and thereby weakening the German strength in the western theatre of war. But this aim degenerated into an inefficient and poorly planned attempt at crushing Bolshevism in its early stages. In June 1919 Sherwood-Kelly uncharacteristically not only failed to press home an attack on a Bolshevik-held position but also withdrew his troops. In a recently published book dealing with the Allied war in Russia at this time a portrait of Sherwood-Kelly emerges not of a man whose mental faculties had been disturbed by five years of fighting as was felt by some at the time, but of a front line officer leading his troops into further but this time futile sacrifices.[13]

Having continued to protest, in writing, to his superior officers and to his friends about the expedition he was eventually relieved of his command in August. This personal stand, although admirable in the front line, was continued by Sherwood-Kelly in September with a scathing attack on British policies and methods in Russia in a letter to the *Daily Express* and from then he became a personality of national interest. The War Office, led by Winston Churchill was now challenged to justify their actions, which Sherwood-Kelly now claimed to include large scale offensive operations against the Bolsheviks. Questions in the House were aimed at Churchill who continued to claim that all operations were designed to cover the withdrawal of the main force from Russia. Support for Sherwood-Kelly grew but the Army took direct action by summoning him to a Court Martial for 'contravening the King's Regulations by writing three letters to the press'.

At the Middlesex Guildhall on 28 October he pleaded guilty as charged. He defended his actions by saying 'I plead with you to believe that the action I took was to protect my men's lives against needless sacrifice and to save the country from squandering wealth she could ill afford. I leave this matter in your hands, hoping that you will remember my past services to my King and country.'[14] With a severe reprimand he recognised that this was the end of his military career and he retired a few weeks later. There is evidence to suggest that Churchill did want an offensively orientated campaign as Sherwood-Kelly claimed but at the same time Lloyd George had already issued instructions for the withdrawal of troops via Archangel.

Post-war life was beset with more problems and failures for Sherwood-Kelly as he failed to get elected to Parliament and also to revive his military career. He died in 1931 at the age of 51 in a nursing home. At his funeral he received full military honours including two buglers sent by the Army to sound the Last Post over his grave.

Not for the first time men from Norfolk and Suffolk went on to inspire the nation into greater efforts and epitomised the strong loyalty felt by many provincial counties to the nation. Some were regular soldiers well aware of the dangers of rash and daring deeds, while others had limited experience perhaps of only a few months. But two things they did have in common. Whether experienced or otherwise no one could predict the horrors that four years of trench warfare and new weapons would create, nor their own reactions to a peculiar set of circumstances that they alone would be a part of.

No doubt thousands of individual acts of extreme sacrifice and heroism went unnoticed among the mud and destruction of the battlefields but some were recognised to be of the highest order and rewarded with the Victoria Cross and all that went with it. There was no single rule book for recommendation for the award. Often it was purely personal impressions and emotion that led senior officers to record their feelings on the actions of those under their command. What was worthy of a recommendation in one section of the battlefield would perhaps have been lost in a wave of such actions in another. Therefore it was often with some surprise that soldiers learnt of their award. To have survived was enough.

Without doubt in the short term many lives were changed by the recognition that the V.C. brought with it. In the longer term however this fame reverted to the recipient's home town or county where they are still remembered. Generalisations are dangerous but the N.C.O. grade dominates this particular group of awards, perhaps illustrative of the high expectation and responsibilities placed on these ranks in the British Army. Post-war experiences are not easy to trace but certainly assimilation back into civilian society was often without support and very soon they had to be reliant on their educational and social background to survive in peacetime.

But their individual deeds stand on their own in any age as examples of what sacrifies were made in the war. For thousands of other servicemen the Military Cross or Military Medal paid tribute to this while for an élite few came immortality with the award of the Victoria Cross.

Notes

1. Figures from *Ribbons and Medals*, by Capt. T. Dorling (George Philip & Son, 1970).
2. See 'The Flowerdew Saga', *The Framlinghamian* for 1960–61.
3. *Eastern Daily Press*, 10 January 1970.
4. Ibid., 9 April 1987.
5. *London Gazette*, 17 October 1917.
6. *Eastern Daily Press*, 1929.
7. See also an article in the *East Anglian Daily Times*, 11 September 1985, by Mr H. Double.
8. *Lowestoft Journal*, 1 August 1986.
9. *The History of the Suffolk Regiment, 1914–1927*, by Lt. Col. C. C. R. Murphy (Hutchinson).
10. *Eastern Daily Press*, December 1978.
11. *The Victoria Cross* by General Sir O'Moore Creagh, V.C., G.C.B., and Miss E. M. Humphries.
12. *Eastern Daily Press* archives.
13. *The Day We Almost Bombed Moscow*, by John Miller and Christopher Dobson (Hodder & Stoughton, 1986), pp. 204–08.
14. Ibid., p. 207.

Lavenham – One Town's Sacrifice

by
Gerald Gliddon

The former wool town of Lavenham in Suffolk lies south-east of Bury St Edmunds and west of Ipswich. The town became prosperous through its wool trade which lasted for virtually six hundred years, and at the beginning of the twentieth century this trade still provided the town with its main source of employment. One particular large employer was W. W. Roper who produced horsehair seating and coconut fibre matting. Ropers employed 356 people and another large employer was a brick factory. The town was still quite prosperous in the period leading up to the beginning of the Great War. The population only declined slightly from 2,016 in 1901 to 1,963 in 1911. In 1914 the population was probably in the region of 1,900 to 2,000.

The Territorial Reserve had been formed nationally in Britain in 1908 and its main function was to provide a support to the regular army which at that time was very small. The likely European aggressor was considered to be Germany with its aims of territorial expansion and industrial progress.

When war was declared on 4 August 1914 it was the Territorials who were immediately called up by the War Office in order to give support to the British Expeditionary Force which was being got ready to go overseas immediately. The instructions for the Lavenham Territorials were to come from Whitehall via the local Post Office which was due to stay open all night especially. The orders arrived at midnight and each Territorial's house was visited and each soldier was told to make himself ready and to attend a meeting that was to take place in the Market Place.

It was not at first thought that the war would last beyond Christmas and the British Territorials treated the whole business as a sort of big adventure. Almost alone it was Kitchener who thought otherwise about the possible length of the war and he immediately set about forming a massive Volunteer Army which would provide men to serve with the already committed professional Army as well as the Territorials. It was to be 1917 before conscription was brought in as a necessity in order to increase the numbers of men in the services, which had been severely depleted by the battle of the Somme in particular. The main substance of this chapter on Lavenham, and its role in the First World War, is taken from the Memorial

Book that is part of the Lavenham Church War Memorial to those who died in the war. It was compiled by G. H. Lenox-Conyngham who was Rector of the town from 1917 until 1933. He obviously felt that just a list of names on a memorial stone would not be sufficient and decided to write short biographies of the men of the town who gave their lives. The writer of this chapter has never come across a memorial similar to this one in Britain.

The book gives brief service histories of each man together with details of their deaths and the Rector often quotes from officers, chaplains or colleagues who knew the men before they died. The Rector must have visited each family in order to obtain this information, and it is hardly surprising that sometimes the dates and battalion number are not always the same as those given in the official listing that was issued after the war was over and which is called *Soldiers Died in the Great War*.

The Rector wrote that between four and five hundred men from Lavenham took part in the war and that there were very few able bodied men left in the town. Those who were left were either too old to fight, or medically unfit, or in reserve occupations. Maybe unemployment and poverty were inducements to this almost wholesale joining up. It would certainly contribute to the high percentage of war deaths in the town with seventy-six men dying out of the four or five hundred who joined the services.

As already said, it was the Territorials who were the first to come forward and they met in the Market Place within a few hours of war being declared. The Market Place was the natural meeting centre of the town and had been for hundreds of years. Fairs and markets had been held there since the thirteenth century and at one time it was even used for bull baiting. Of the seventy-six men who died fourteen were members of the Territorials although of course the Market Place meeting would have had many more than just fourteen men.

It would be useful at this stage to give a breakdown of just which regimental units the seventy-six joined. I will always try and give the last unit of which they were members and so if they began with one Regiment or Battalion and transferred to another it is the second one that I have used. If the dates quoted differ I will put the 'official date' in brackets. Of the seventy-six, not surprisingly as many as thirty-six were members of nine Suffolk battalions. Another twenty-eight were to join other infantry battalions including the Essex, Lincolns, King's Shropshire Light Infantry, King's Liverpool, Norfolk, Northumberland Fusiliers, Northamptonshires, Queen's Royal West Kents, Duke of Wellingtons, Royal Warwickshires, West Yorkshires, Bedfords, Middlesex, Royal Fusiliers, the Coldstream Guards, and the Canadian Infantry. In addition six served with either the Royal Field Artillery or the Royal Garrison Artillery. One man was with the Royal Army Medical Corps, one with the Royal Naval Division and three with the Machine Gun Corps. This is a very wide spread of units but pretty typical of the way that the Army was organised during the war. One man served in the Royal Navy.

Of the Suffolks, eleven joined the 5th Battalion, eight the 2nd, and the other seventeen were spread over seven other Suffolk Battalions.

Because there were so few men left in Lavenham during the war the jobs that had fallen vacant were taken over by women. They worked in the local factories, including munitions and in farms, shops, hospitals, etc.

The first Lavenham man to be reported killed was **Private Arthur Welham** of Water Street who enlisted with the Suffolks in 1906 serving in Malta and Egypt. When the war began he was with the Essex Mounted Police. He then rejoined his Regiment in Ireland and went to France on 15 August 1914. He was reported missing during the retreat from Mons in Belgium on 26 August when the 2nd Suffolks were overwhelmed at Le Cateau, while acting as a rearguard to the 5th Division. Less than a hundred men survived from this action. Ten other men from Water Street in addition to Welham were to lose their lives in the war.

It was to be February 1915 before Lavenham was to lose another of its sons and 1915 as a whole was to be the least costly in terms of men's lives in that only eleven out of seventy-six were to die.

Charles Benstead of 37 High Street, who was probably related to the local Police Inspector H. G. Benstead, enlisted in the 1st Suffolks in 1906 and rose to the rank of Sergeant, Benstead was in Khartoum when war broke out and returned to England in November 1914 before going to France in January. He was killed on 16 February when he was bringing in two wounded men, and having rescued the first was shot in the hand when bringing in the second man. He was killed as he reached the trench.

Private Walter Curtis of 5 Pump Street was with the 1st Suffolks and had been in Egypt when war broke out. He went to France in February and was killed on 16 March. The soldiers that he was with were parched with thirst and Curtis collected water for them twice and was killed when going out for the third time.

James Cecil Carter of 56b High Street enlisted with the Royal Fusiliers on 14 November 1914 and trained at the White City before going to France in February. He fought at Neuve Chapelle and on 9 May was told to take a trench which was in enemy hands. He was seriously wounded in the attack on the trench and 'bore his pain like a hero' and died later in the day on 13 May.

Private Charles Parker lived next door to James Carter at 56a High Street and had been in the Militia for nine years before joining the 2nd Suffolks in August 1914. He went to France in the next month and was killed on 11 June. Although 1915 as a full year was not the most disastrous one for the men of Lavenham it was particularly poignant for the men of the 5th Suffolks of whom no less than five from the town were to die by the end of the year. I think it would be appropriate to give a short history of this Territorial Battalion which had its origins as far back as 1859 and had served in the Boer War at the beginning of the century. They were predominantly volunteers at the beginning of the First World War and were not necessarily expecting to go abroad; they were more 'Saturday Night Soldiers'. Nevertheless as many as seventy-two per cent volunteered for overseas service. They trained in various parts of England and entrained from Watford at the end of July 1915 bound for Liverpool, where they boarded a large liner called H.M.T. *Aquitaine* which had to steer a zig zag course in order to avoid enemy submarines. Eventually the ship reached Mudros harbour in the island of Lemnos. The Suffolks were bound for the Gallipoli Peninsula. They remained at Mudros for three days before transferring to a smaller ship and proceeding to Imbros Harbour where they landed at Suvla Bay on the south-west side of the Peninsula. In the evening of 10 August they were ordered up to dig trenches to the right of the Lancashire Fusiliers on the south side of a position called Karakol Dagh, thus filling in a gap between it and the north-east edge of Salt Lake (a dry lake during the summer months). Two days later on 12 August the Suffolks were given orders to advance 1,200 yards towards the Turkish lines in a due east direction. The battalion to their right was the 5th Norfolks with the 8th Hampshires in the centre and the Suffolks on the left directing the attack. The Suffolks had no Field Artillery to support them as it had not come with them to the Peninsula but they were protected to some extent by naval guns from the sea. Apart from the fighting the general conditions were very trying and water was in short supply continuously. The attack lasted for seventy hours before relief.

On 12 August **Private William Smith** was reported missing at Suvla Bay. He had lived at 72 Water Street and had been one of the Territorials called up on 4 August 1914. He had trained at Colchester and marched from there to Bury St Edmunds before staying one night at Lavenham.

The *History of the 1/5 Battalion The Suffolk Regiment* by Captains A. Fair and E. D. Wolton gives a detailed account of the Gallipoli campaign and the Wolton family address was The Hall, Lavenham. **2nd. Lt. O. B. Wolton** was a member of 'C' Company, Lt. H. C. Wolton was with 'D' Company and Lt. E. D. Wolton was not involved in the August fighting but was later to be wounded in October.

Owen Biddell Wolton had been a member of the Loyal Suffolk Hussars from 1910 and mobilised in August 1914. He too was reported missing after the landing at Suvla Bay, but nevertheless has a memorial in Lavenham Churchyard. On the same day (12 August) **Private Frederick Sturgeon** of Hall Road was killed at a point called Hill 60 Anzac. In Kelly's *Directory* there is a mention of F. R. Sturgeon as being Farm Bailiff to Cordy S. Wolton, one of the larger farmers of Lavenham. Sturgeon is one of several men where there appears to be a difference in the date of death – Lenon-Conyngham says that he died on 12 August and the official volume says that he died of wounds on 11 September.

On 15 (21) August on the third day of the Suffolks' attack against the Turks **Private George Twitchett** was reported missing. The Rector reported that Twitchett's mother died of a broken heart as a result of her son's death. Twitchett too had been one of the pre-war Territorials. A few days later the fifth member of the 5th Suffolks' contingent from Lavenham was to die on the Peninsula. **Private James Aldous** of Acton Road was wounded in the reserve trenches on 22 August and died of wounds the next day.

It was in September and October when another battle that was to prove to be disastrous to the British was fought in France. It was known as the battle of Loos and on 13 October **Private Frederick William Parker** of 8 Market Place was to lose his life at a position called the Hairpin, in an attempt to capture the Hohenzollern Redoubt. Parker had joined the 7th Suffolks in November 1914 and went to France in May. The 7th Suffolks were in the first division of Kitchener's Army to be sent abroad. Parker was probably related to the Lavenham coal dealer who had an address in the Market Place. He was to die in the same fighting as a very famous member of the Suffolk Regiment the poet Charles Sorley, a Captain who died at the age of twenty.

The next Lavenham man to die (chronologically) was another member of the 5th Suffolks on the Gallipoli Peninsula. His name was **Harry Parker** a younger brother of Charles Parker whose address was the same, i.e. 56a High Street. As already stated they lived next door to James Carter at 56b. Harry Parker joined the Suffolks in December 1914 and caught dysentery on the Peninsula, dying on 21 or 22 November. The Rector noted that he was seventeen years of age, which was probably so when he first joined up.

In 1916 fourteen more Lavenham men were to die (three more than in 1915). The first one was **Private Edward Butcher** of Primrose Lane. Butcher enlisted in 1915 and joined the 5th King's Shropshire Light Infantry at Shrewsbury, and went to France in September of that year. He was with a ration party going up to the front line trenches when caught by German machine gun fire. This was on 20 (21) January.

Cpl. Albert Edward Smith of Washmere Green enlisted with the Lincolnshires on 9 September 1914 at Spalding, before going to France he trained on Salisbury Plain. He was a member of the 7th Battalion and came home for six hours in order to see his dying father. He returned to France in July 1915 and took part in the fighting at Ypres in Belgium. In January 1916 he came home for six days and returned again to France in the same month. He was killed on his birthday, 2 March by a shell that killed two and wounded five other men. He was just eighteen.

Private George Lambert of 36 High Street joined the 2nd Suffolks on 23 September 1914 and trained at Felixstowe, Bury St Edmunds and Colchester. He left for France on 27 July 1915 and was wounded near St Eloi with another man. They were both killed by a shell explosion on their way to a dressing station.

Private Thomas Alfred Smith of Sudbury Road enlisted with the Bedfords in July 1915 and went to France in November. He was killed on 13 March when dragging a wounded colleague back from the front trenches. His officer wrote 'Private Smith had done splendid work with the stretcher bearers and more than one of his comrades had reason to be grateful to him. His loss was felt far more by the whole company than for an ordinary Rifleman. His duties required the highest courage and he fulfilled them nobly.'

Driver Ernest Collins aged twenty-three lived at 32 High Street and was a member of the Royal Field Artillery before the war began and was sent to France from India. After some time there he came home for six days' leave. After his death his Lieutenant wrote 'Driver Collins was very highly esteemed by both officers and men of his battery. He was killed instantaneously on 7 June 1917 bringing ammunition to the guns during an attack. The other two drivers were injured and the horses all killed. Your son had distinguished himself on this and on other occasions by his coolness and pluck by bringing ammunition to the guns under fire. He was noted for hard work and the care he bestowed upon his horses. His loss is deplored by the whole battery.' When going to France he left a little money to be kept. While in France he thought his mother was in need and wrote saying 'take all you want, you know where it is'.

Private Frank Steward of 4 Compton Street enlisted with the 21st Canadian Battalion and came to England on his way to France, where he arrived in April 1915. He was killed in Ypres in Belgium on 14 June. His Major wrote 'He was killed with two companions by shell fire in the trenches. He had at all times proved one of my most faithful and courageous men. His cheerful and ever ready disposition endeared him to all his comrades.' He was aged seventeen.

L.Cpl. Thomas Pryke of Market Lane was one of seven brothers to join the Army. He was in the Militia and called up in August 1914. He trained with the 8th Suffolks in Colchester and Felixstowe and went to France in 1914. He was slightly wounded in the shoulder but remained in France. Later he had trench fever and was sent home to recuperate in Manchester Hospital. He spent Christmas at home in 1915, returned to France, was badly wounded and died in hospital on 22 June (2nd Suffolks 22 June 1917).

James Jubilee Kemp lived at 31 Prentice Street. Kemp's middle name of Jubilee probably meant that he was born in the year of Queen Victoria's Diamond Jubilee in 1897. He enlisted in May 1915 and became a gunner with the Royal Garrison Artillery, having trained at Dover. He went to France in June 1916 and was killed on 1 July, the first day of the Battle of the Somme. As a signaller he had obtained highest marks and was killed with two others when resting in a shell hole, the New Testament in his pocket was pierced by a piece of shrapnel.

Private Lewis Sadler of 4 Church Street enlisted in the 10th Suffolks in March 1916 before being transferred to the 2nd Suffolks. He went to France on 20 July and was reported missing on 18 August. He might have been involved in the fighting south-west of Trônes Wood on the Somme, as this is where his battalion was at the time of his death.

Private Thomas Odell Green of a High Street address had been a member of the Territorials and was exempted until November 1915. He joined the Machine Gun Corps and was attached to a London Battalion of the Royal Fusiliers. He had trained with Lewis guns and left for France in March 1916, and was killed on the Somme on 1 October.

Private Frank Alfred Poulson of 24 Water Street enlisted with the 9th Suffolks on 11 January 1915, trained at Brighton and Shorncliffe. In September he went to France and was wounded in the hand by a bayonet in hand to hand fighting at Loos. On 12 October he was in a trench with two Corporals when a shell dropped just in front of them, Poulson was killed, one Corporal was also killed while the third man escaped unhurt. The chaplain wrote 'your son met his death with the true spirit of a British boy and put his duty first and himself second, by that he clasped the full meaning of the faith for which he died'. Poulson could have been taking part in the battle for the Transloy Ridges on the Somme which would tally with the date of his death.

Private Ernest Eady of Hill Farm of the 8th (9th) Suffolks was one of three brothers who all enlisted on the same day in January 1915. They also went to France on the same day. Ernest trained at Brighton and Shorncliffe. He went to France in August 1915, and was disabled by trench feet and sent to hospital in Lincoln. He was placed in the same bed that his brother had been taken from the day before. His brother also had frozen feet. After nearly a year in England he returned to France in September 1916. The three brothers who had become separated in France arranged to meet and it was during this meeting which took place in a trench that Ernest was killed by a shell on 12 October. He was probably killed on the Somme as it would tie in with the death of Frank Poulson.

Private Frederick Thomas Smith of 82 Church Street joined the R.A.M.C. in 1915 when nineteen years of age. He trained at Aldershot and then went to Ireland. From there he went to France arriving there in October 1916. He was the fifth Lavenham man to be killed in the Somme battle which ran from the end of June to 18 November. The chaplain wrote 'he was killed in action on 18 November while in a dugout with two of his chums, by a German shell. The explosion buried the three boys. Your son's body was recovered this morning and laid to rest in the Euston Military Cemetery near Maily. Your boy died while performing the merciful work of rescuing the wounded and in spite of the great sorrow which has come to you, it will be a pride to you that he died as a soldier doing the brave thing.'

The Lavenham man who was killed in 1916 that we know least about is **Private Frank Knock** of 51 High Street who joined the Suffolks in November 1914 and was transferred to the Northumberland Fusiliers. He went to France in August 1916 and was killed on 19 November. He might have been killed on the Somme or elsewhere on the Westen Front.

Although 1916 on the Somme had been the year traditionally associated with very high casualties it was in fact 1917 which was to be the most disastrous for the people of Lavenham and of the seventy-six who were to die throughout the war nearly a third (i.e. twenty-five) were to die in this single year. High points of the battle on the Western Front in this year, when both sides had reached a stalemate, were the battles of Arras which took place in April, the battle of Messines Ridge in June and the still frequently debated third battle of Ypres better known as the battle of Passchendaele.

In his pamphlet called *Lavenham in War Time 1914–1918* the Rector wrote 'The name of every soldier from Lavenham, who gave his life for his country, was read out from the pulpit on the Sunday after his death was known, and the muffled bells were rung as a mark of respect. Few will forget the awe-stricken hush through the church as Sunday after Sunday these names were read.'

As if it was a sorrowful sign of things to come a Lavenham man was even killed on 1 January of the new year and his name was **Private Frank Wheeler** of 1 High Street which was and still is the butcher's shop (1988). He was one of six brothers who joined the Army. He had just gone out to Canada where he volunteered in February 1915, and trained with the 75th Canadians. He went to France in November 1916 and was killed when going out to repair a trench at 7 p.m. which the Germans had blown up the night before. Thirteen men were walking in single file when a shell fell killing nine of them. His friend who was unhurt went to him and said 'Are you hurt Frank?' The answer was 'they've got me this time'. His friend took off Frank's knapsack and put it under his head, went and did the same for another man and then came back to Frank who asked how soon the ambulance would be and died as he was speaking.

Private Arthur William Partridge of 28 Bolton Street enlisted in the 7th Suffolks in August 1914. He was so determined to enlist that there was no holding him back. He walked to Melford on the Sunday, slept there, walked to Sudbury on the Monday but was found to be too narrow in the chest. The next Thursday he walked to Bury St Edmunds and was passed. He trained at Shorncliffe and went to France on 31 May. He fought at Festubert, Neuve Chapelle, Kemmel Hill, Ploegsteert Wood, Lens, Vimy Ridge, Bethune, Hulloch Quarries, Vermelles, Houplines, Armentières, Laventie and Loos. He was a member of the 7th Suffolks but was serving with the 176th Company Royal Engineers when he was killed on 11 January. His Captain wrote 'he was killed while on duty at 2 p.m. on 11 January 1917, his death being instantaneous. Please accept the sincerest sympathy of officers, N.C.O.s. and men of his section. In his death we have lost a gallant soldier who was always cheerful, ready to do his duty. I have known him personally for some months and feel his loss more than I can say. He was buried this morning with military honours behind the firing line.'

The next man from Bolton Street to be killed was **Joseph Hunt** of number 11. He joined the 5th Suffolks when only sixteen and trained for a year and nine months before transferring to the Norfolk Regiment. He went out to France on 3 December 1916 and died just over two months later on 16 February. He was killed while going out through no-man's-land with a Lewis gun and was buried at Grandcourt (on the Somme). His Sergeant wrote 'he was killed while trying to reach the front line with a carrying party and they came under heavy fire and died almost immediately. I must say that while he was with us he was always a brave happy little fellow and I miss him very much.' His Sergeant wrote this when just out of the line. Six weeks later the Sergeant himself was killed.

Eight days later **Private Alexander Bert Twitchett**, of The Common (which is at the bottom of Water Street), died having been wounded on 19 February. He had joined the 10th Royal Fusiliers in June 1916 and went to France in September 1916.

Cpl. Edward Thomas Poulson of 20 Market Place was a Territorial when called up on 4 August 1914, and was attached to the 1st Suffolks. He went to France in 1916 and was wounded when shot in the shoulder on 8 March 1917. At this time he is listed as being with the 5th Suffolks (the Regimental History does not tally with the circumstances of his being wounded). He was taken to Hospital in Scotland on 9 March and died there on 15 March. He is buried in Lavenham Churchyard.

The next three men to die were all killed in April and it is fair to assume that they were all taking part in the battle of Arras whose dates were from 9 April–3 May. It was during this period of fighting that British and Colonial troops took Vimy Ridge.

Another member of the **Poulson** family **Private Frederick G.** had enlisted with the 27th Middlesex Battalion then transferred to 23rd Reserve Brigade School and qualified as a Signaller. On 13 December 1916 he left for France and became a member of the 4th Royal Fusiliers. He was killed on 9 April the first day of the battle of Arras.

Private Reginald William Smith of 38 Prentice Street joined the 7th

Northamptonshire Battalion in August 1916 and went to France in December of that year. He was killed on 17 April near Arras.

The next day the third Arras casualty **Lance Cpl. George Knock** of 58 High Street was killed. He had been with the Suffolks before the war and was in Egypt when the war began. He went to France with the Bedfords in February 1915 and was invalided home with wounds on three occasions. Once with frozen feet when he was unable to walk for many months.

Robert Charles Middleton Harper of The Priory in Water Street was one of only two officers from the list of Lavenham war dead. He had begun his service in the ranks. He enlisted in the 5th Suffolks when the detachment was formed in Lavenham in March 1912. They were mobilised on the outbreak of war. He left England on 29 July 1915 and was present at the landings at Suvla Bay on the Gallipoli Peninsula where we have seen already that five men from his battalion were not to return. He escaped this tragedy and in early 1917 accepted a commission with the 5th Norfolks. It was while serving with them that he was reported missing in the second battle of Gaza in Palestine on 19 April. As a boy he had won a scholarship to the West Suffolk County School at Bury St Edmunds and returned as assistant master at Lavenham Council School. He was also a member of the church choir and of the string band. In October 1915 he had been promoted to the rank of Company Quarter Master Sergeant and remained with the Suffolks in the Egyptian Desert during 1916. In January 1917 he obtained his commission in the 1/5th Norfolks, having passed among the first of the cadets. He had much organising ability and on one occasion he greatly assisted in getting the transport out of a muddle and he had also taken part in the first battle of Gaza in March 1917 and in the second in April when he was reported missing. His Company Commander wrote of him 'he was one of the best N.C.O.s I ever had as he was so invariably cheerful, quick and obliging. He was popular with the men who would do anything for him, as C.Q.M.S. on the Peninsula in 1915 he did great work looking after the men's welfare, at a time when comforts were absolutely minimal. As an officer I knew he made an excellent beginning and I am sure that his premature death cut short a very promising career.'

Private Sydney Eary of Hall Road had first worked in the Labour Corps in France in 1915 where he was wounded and sent home. He then joined the 15th West Yorkshires and was reported killed on 3 May which was the last day of the battle of Arras. At one point he had been buried for four days without food in a dugout.

Three days later on 6 May **Private William James Carter** of the Market Place was killed in action. He was a member of the 12th Suffolks. *Soldiers Died* volume records his being killed in action in France on 6 May, but the Rector wrote 'he went to France and was wounded and made prisoner and then sent to Switzerland where he died'.

108

Private Frederick Wheeler of the butcher's shop at number 1 High Street was one of six brothers who had joined the Army. He enlisted in the Royal Fusiliers in 1915, and went to France in 1916. He was killed on 17 June 1917 but we don't know where. He was in a shell hole close to the German line throwing bombs when a shell came over and burst in the very shell hole where he was and blew him to pieces. He left a wife and three children.

Private George Eliston of the Market Place enlisted with the 8th Bedfords on 30 May 1916 and trained at Landguard near Felixstowe before going to France in September 1916. When there, he was severely wounded in the knee by shrapnel and was sent home to hospital at Westcliff on Sea. He came home to Lavenham for a short time and was then sent to Felixstowe. He then returned to France and was killed in action on 25 June.

Private Alfred Ernest Anderson of the Swan Inn joined the Hussars in 1910 and was training at the School of Music, Neller Hall when war broke out. He was ordered to rejoin his Regiment and went to France with the Cavalry of the Machine Gun Corps in September 1915. He was hurt in an accident and returned to England. He then went to Mesopotamia as Colonel's Trumpeter in March 1917 and died there of fever on 19 July.

Private John Ambrose of Bolton Street enlisted in the Suffolks in July 1915. He trained at Dovercourt and went to France on 2 December 1916. He was given leave twice and might have had a third leave but gave it up to another soldier whose wife was ill. In France he was for nine days in a dugout he couldn't leave as it was shelled continuously the whole time. In France he sprained his foot and was sent to a rest camp, an officer giving him his horse to ride to the camp. He was killed the very day he returned to the front. On Christmas Eve he was saying how different was the service there held in a barn from the services in the beautiful church at home. The chaplain wrote 'he was much liked by all his comrades and most regular in his attendance at all services. He was killed instantaneously and buried where he fell. There is some doubt about his place of burial. A comrade wrote that he had found the body three weeks later with a letter from his wife beside it and then buried him near Sanctuary Wood. Ambrose was with the 8th Suffolks and was killed on 31 July, which was the first day of the third battle of Ypres.

Private Arthur Henry Poulson aged thirty-one of 4 Prospect View enlisted in the Suffolks in October 1915, transferred to the King's Liverpool Regiment and trained at Felixstowe. He went to France on 3 January 1917, was gassed and sent to hospital in France. On leaving hospital he was sent to St Quentin where he was wounded on 31 July, he was taken again to hospital and died on 9 August. His Lieutenant wrote 'that our stretcher bearers were busy at the time and he was carried by bearers from another battalion, consequently he did not pass through our lines and we have no trace of him. While your son was with us he always set a fine example of unfailing cheerfulness and devotion to duty, and I can only assure you that we are all very sorry to lose him from our midst.'

Private Frederick George Smith of 6 Pyghthe Terrace enlisted in the Suffolks in 1915 and trained at Bury St Edmunds and Stowlangtont(?). He went to France in June 1917 and was killed in Belgium on 17 August. He is said to have been with the 5th Suffolks who were not in the area at that time so he was probably killed at the start of the third battle of Ypres when attached to another Suffolk Battalion.

Private Arthur James Eady of 22 Prentice Street joined the West Yorkshires and went to France in May 1917 and was killed five months later in October.

William John Argent of 32 Church Street was the only one of Lavenham's dead from the First World War who died while serving with the Royal Navy, which he joined on 21 December 1915. He entered the Royal Navy Barracks at Devonport and in April 1916 joined H.M.S. *Brisk* which was a ship designed to hunt enemy submarines. The ship was attached to the Second Destroyer Flotilla, engaged in not only attacking enemy submarines but also in escorting troopships up channel to France. In February 1917 he was involved in the rescue of troops who were on board S.S. *Menin* which had been in collision with another troopship and was sunk off Southampton. The troops lost were South African labour corps troops, and 600 were lost. The accident happened through fog and H.M.S. *Brisk* was the escort vessel. In April it had sunk an enemy submarine. On 2 October while engaged in escorting a convoy of forty ships across the Atlantic H.M.S. *Drake* was attacked by submarines and sunk off Ratting Island off the north coast of Ireland. H.M.S. *Brisk* proceeded to her assistance and was attacked by five submarines and sunk.

Private William Rampling who was probably connected with the Boot and Shoe shop in Barn Street, joined the Territorials at the age of seventeen in Skipton, Yorkshire. He was attached to the 1/6 Duke of Wellingtons and went to France from Doncaster on 12 April 1915, having crossed from Southampton to Le Havre on the night of 13 April. Nearly six months later he was killed on the Passchendaele Ridge at a point east of St Julien, north-west of Zonnebeke, north-east of Ypres on 9 October.

Private William George Munnings of Melford Road joined the 9th Suffolks in August 1914, trained at Bury St Edmunds and Aldershot and went to France in April 1915. By this time I think that he had joined the 7th Suffolks. In May he was wounded in both legs and was in hospital in England for three months. He went home to Lavenham for six weeks and returned to France in November 1915. He was killed nearly two years later on 14 October 1917.

Private Thomas Harold Bruce of 37 Prentice Street joined the Lancers on 5 September 1914, and transferred to the 9th Lancers and went to France in

June 1916. He was invalided home in September 1916 and returned to France four months later in January 1917. He was again invalided home and kept in hospital under October 1917. He then joined the 14th Royal Warwicks to go into the firing line and wrote home on 25 October the day before he died. He reported that he was out of the firing line without a scratch but had lost all his belongings. The next day he was reported missing.

Private Ernest George Poulson of 20 Market Place, aged seventeen was probably a younger brother of Cpl. Edward Thomas Poulson of the same address who had died in March of the same year. Ernest too was a member of the Territorials and was called up on 4 August 1914. He sailed to Gallipoli with the ill fated 5th Suffolks and took part in the third battle of Gaza in Palestine, and was killed on 2 November. He was buried in a military cemetery at Gaza. The 5th Suffolks were to lose two more Lavenham men and the first one was **Private Charles Sadler** of 16 Prentice Street, who also began in 1914 with the Territorials and went to Gallipoli in 1915, taking part in the landings at Suvla Bay in August 1915. He too was killed in the third battle of Gaza on the same day as Ernest Poulson, on 2 November. It was said that he always wrote home very regularly and made light of his hardships. 'We think nothing of aeroplanes here, one will soon be coming to look in my pocket to see the time.' He had voluntarily relinquished the comparatively safe role of a guide to the camel convoys, preferring to take part with his friends in the front line.

The last Lavenham man to die in the Middle East in 1917 was **Private George Pryke** of 33 Church Street. He was one of seven brothers who joined the Army. He himself joined the 5th Suffolks in January 1915, and sailed to Gallipoli with the rest of his battalion. He also fought in Palestine and died of dysentery at Port Said on 5 December. 'Officers and men spoke of him as a thorough good sort and you cannot have a better tribute. He was a quiet conscientious worker and I have never heard a word against him.'

If 1917 had been a very sad year for the people of Lavenham with the deaths of twenty-five of its sons then 1918 was to be only a marginal improvement, with the loss of twenty-two men. It was a curious fact that in what was to be the last year of the war, that as many as twelve different units were represented by these twenty-two Lavenham men, of which four were Suffolk battalions. There is no real pattern to the deaths and there were no set piece battles. After the famous German March breakthrough the Allies were considered to be slowly winning from early August onwards. However two-thirds of the 1918 deaths occurred *after* this date which suggests an over zealous attacking strategy. In other words the enemy was on the retreat, it was just a question of time, there was really no need to squander lives. The authorities too were prepared for the war to go on into the next year. On the other side of the argument it could be stated that lives were saved through this rapid Allied advance.

We have very little information about **Cpl. Richard Welham** of 12 Prentice Street who had been in the Suffolk Regiment for some years before the war began, when he was sent to France. He was a member of the 11th Suffolks and *Soldiers Died* lists him as being a casualty on 22 March 1918.

Private Eleazer Hartley of 21 Bolton Street, who was probably related to Joseph Hartley who ran a local carrier service, was the next Lavenham man to die. He had enlisted in the 2nd Suffolks in December 1914 and trained at Felixstowe before going to France in April 1915. In the following month he was wounded in the wrist by a bullet and sent to hospital in England. He returned to France in October. A year later he was wounded again by a bullet but this time in the shoulder. He returned home and was sent to hospital in Wales. While recuperating he worked on the land until he was fit for service. He returned to France in April 1917. He came home on leave in March 1918 and returned to France only to be reported missing on 28 March.

Sgt. Reginald Faiers of 5 Hall Road, a house very close to the church began his service with the Territorials on 4 August 1914, and trained recruits in England as a gymnastic instructor. He became a Sergeant and went to France on 4 December 1917 and was wounded in March 1918 and taken to Hospital at Etaples, the principal training base in France for British troops. He died there on 29 March. He is said to have gone forward to ask some Germans to surrender and to have been shot down by them. He was with the 7th Suffolks and the battles at the time of his death were the battles for the Albert bridgeheads in the second battle of the Somme.

Private Charles Albert Capon of 74 Church Street was one of six members of the Lavenham dead who was a member of the Royal Artillery. He was a Gunner with the Royal Field Artillery, and had joined up on 9 July 1917 and went to France on 21 November 1917. He was killed on 9 April 1918.

Private John Richard Sadler of 16 Prentice Street began his service with the Territorials on 4 August 1914 and joined the Duke of Wellingtons in March 1916. He went to France in May of that year and was wounded slightly in July 1916. He came home for a short leave and returned to France again in September 1916. He was reported missing while serving with the Machine Gun Corps on 13 April. He had been given a bronze medallion for rifle shooting.

Charles Harold Eady of 22 Prentice Street was a Gunner with the Royal Field Artillery and went to France in October 1917. He was killed on 30 (29) April 1918. His Major wrote 'he was struck by a shell and killed. His end was quite painless. He was much loved by us all. Although he had been in the battery a comparatively short time the quiet way in which he did his duty and did it well made him much admire by his comrades and officers.'

Perhaps the unluckiest man from Lavenham to be killed was **Alfred John**

Smith of 17 Prentice Street. He had enlisted in the Norfolks on 27 July 1916 and trained at Felixstowe and was transferred to the Machine Gun Corps. He went to France on 27 December 1916. He was gassed at St Quentin and was three times in hospital there. He came home on leave in January 1918 and was taken prisoner on the Somme on 21 March 1918. This would have been a result of the German breakthrough. He was sent as a prisoner to the village of Ham and there killed by a bomb dropped by a French airman on 6 June. When he had come home on leave he had arrived at 11.30 p.m. unexpectedly as it was the Sergeant's turn for leave but he said, 'Smith has been out longer so he shall have it.' No news was received about him from the time he was reported missing until the week after the Armistice when the news came that he had been killed.

Private Charles William Pryke of 33 Church Street joined the 3rd Suffolks on 7 July 1915 when sixteen years of age and trained at Felixstowe for three years before going to France on 2 April 1918. He had probably transferred to the 2nd Suffolks as the 3rd Battalion were not abroad at the time of his death. He was wounded on 27 June and taken to a Canadian Casualty Clearing Station and then to Vimereux Hospital on 28 June. He suffered from shell wounds and also gas gangrene infection. He died on 10 July. In hospital 'he was bright, brave and cheerful and comes from a splendid fighting family and is a fine lad himself'.

Able Seaman William Charles Knock of 41 Prentice Street joined the Royal Naval Division when eighteen years old. The R.N.D. was the Admiralty's contribution to the Army and its Divisional number was 63. Knock went to France in June 1917 and was wounded and gassed. He returned to England on 19 January 1918 and went back to France in June. He was killed on 25 August.

Private Percy Long of Lower Road joined the 3rd Suffolks in July 1915 when sixteen years old and trained at Felixstowe. He went to France on 12 September 1917 having transferred to the West Riding Regiment. He was wounded on 26 August 1918 and died on the way from the Dressing Station to the Clearing Station.

Private Albert Charles Faiers of 9 Shilling Street joined the 2nd Suffolks in July 1916 when sixteen and trained at Felixstowe. He left for France on 28 March and was wounded on 21 August. He died sixteen days later on 6 September and was buried at Le Tréport. He might have been taking part in the second battle of the Somme.

Private Bertram Jarvis of 36 Prentice Street, joined the 6th Royal West Kents in August 1915 and went to France four months later in December. He was wounded in 1916 and was in hospital in France for some months. He was killed on 21 September.

Private Richard Mills of 12 Water Street joined the 1st Suffolks in June 1915 when he too was sixteen and trained at Felixstowe until he was

113

nineteen. He then transferred to the 10th Essex and went to France on Easter Sunday March 1918. He was killed on 21 September.

Mills' next door neighbour at 11 Water Street was **Cpl. James Ambrose** who joined the Territorials on 4 August 1914. He transferred to the 1/8 Royal Warwicks and went to France in 1916. He was invalided home with frozen feet and went back to France in 1917. He was soon sent to the Italian Front and remained there for ten months, before returning to France where he was killed on 6 October.

L.Cpl. Charles Dakin of Sudbury Road enlisted on 24 June 1916 in the Royal Fusiliers and trained in Edinburgh before going to France on 8 October 1916. He received gunshot wounds at Arras on 3 May 1917 and was sent to recover at Liverpool Hospital. He went back to France in July 1917 and was wounded again on 11 October 1918 and died the next day. His officer wrote 'his loss will be greatly felt by myself, the officers, N.C.O.s and men of the Company. I can ill afford to lose such a gallant and conscientious commissioned officer. He was extremely popular with all ranks. His gallantry in action was the admiration of them all. He was hit while engaging a nest of hostile machine guns and his leadership of his Lewis gun team was largely responsible for the silencing of this nest. Thus enabling our advance to be continued.' He was buried near Cambrai, which had been captured on 9 October.

Private Charles Henry Poulson of 9 Water Street joined the 26th Royal Fusiliers on 21 May 1917 when eighteen years old. After his training he came home on leave before starting for France and was only home for a day when a telegram came recalling him to his Regiment to start at once for France. He was killed on 14 October 1918.

Gunner William Edward Young lived in the High Street and enlisted in the Royal Field Artillery on 18 October 1916. The next year he went to France and was blown up there and his back injured. He was sent to Hospital in Oxford and went to Italy in 1918, only to be blown to pieces in a dugout on 24 October. His remains were buried at the British Military Cemetery at Maserad Treviso. He was the only Lavenham man to be killed in Italy in a campaign which is often overlooked.

Private Harold Benjamin Lester of 9 Bolton Street enlisted in the 1st Suffolks on 10 July 1915 when sixteen years old. He acted as a Drummer while training at Felixstowe and was transferred to the Machine Gun Corps. He went to France in June 1918 and was killed in the last month of the war on 1 November. His body was buried in an isolated grave at a crossroads near Courtrai. His N.C.O. wrote 'he was my best soldier and my most experienced gunner'. The chaplain wrote 'he was one of the most delightful boys I have come across'.

L.Cpl. Rossiter Rudd of Water Street joined the 13th Middlesex Battalion at the age of twenty-seven on 29 May 1916. He trained at

Chatham for a year and went to France in March 1917. He was ill in hospital at Le Tréport from March to September 1918 and was killed by a shell at Villers Pol on 4 November. His Major wrote 'he was killed during the advance. I went to the spot but could not do anything as we had received orders to go on. I had formed a very high opinion of him indeed and he proved a very useful man to me. He was a comrade we all liked, his word was his bond.' Rudd was probably related to the Rudd who ran a fish shop in Lavenham. The Armistice was signed on 11 November and one would have thought that the deaths would have ended there. Unfortunately this was not to be and there were no fewer than five more deaths of men from Lavenham within a whole year of the war being declared finished.

On 11 November in Lavenham a service was arranged to commemorate the signing of the Armistice and the Rector wrote the following:

'The news of the signing came early, and such a thrill of joy filled every heart as had not been felt for over four years. The houses were decorated and the bells were rung, and it was arranged to hold a Thanksgiving Service in the Church in the evening. The Church which had not been lighted up for some years, was lighted up again, and all denominations joined in the Service. There was a congregation of nearly twelve hundred people at 7.30 p.m.'

The procession was formed in the Market Place. Headed by the Salvation Army Band, the parade, including soldiers, women-workers, the Suffolk Volunteer Regiment, No. 3 Platoon, under Lieut. J. Cutts, the Boy Scouts, under Scoutmaster Miss Lenox-Conyngham marched to the Church. The body of the Church was reserved for those who formed the procession, the V.A.D.s, and the Parish Council. The sermon was preached by the Rector, the Rev. G. H. Lenox-Conyngham.

The last member of the Royal Artillery to die was **Driver William Frederick Smith** of Prospect View who had enlisted in the Royal Field Artillery on 18 January 1915, and trained at Aldershot before going to France in June 1915. He was never wounded although horses were shot from under him several times. On 10 November he was coming home on leave, the night before the Armistice, caught cold on the voyage, which developed into pneumonia. He died on 15 November at Mile End Hospital, north of Colchester.

Private Walter Eary of Hall Road joined the Duke of Wellingtons in 1915 and went to France in 1916. He served in Italy and was invalided home and died at Leeds Hospital on 19 November 1918.

Private Frederick Smith of 8 Prentice Street was a member of the Reserve and as such was called up to join the 2nd Suffolks when the war began. He went to France in 1917 after being stationed at Stowmarket. He was taken prisoner on 28 March 1918 and came home extremely weakened by lack of food and was sent to Sudbury Hospital where he died on 11 December 1918.

William H. Welham was the only Lavenham man to die as a member of the Guards and he served with the Coldstreams in France, but died of spotted fever in Felixstowe at a date unknown. He lived in Water Street.

The very last two men to die as a result of the war died one year after the war officially ended and they were **Pte Percy Hughes** of 14 Shilling Street who enlisted under the Derby scheme and was called up in August 1916 with the Middlesex Regiment. He trained at Norwich and while training he had to go into hospital twice and was declared unfit for foreign service. He was transferred to the Labour Corps. He spent six months in Lavenham and was then sent to Ipswich where he died on 13 November 1919. He had spent some time at home on the land.

Private George Dent died on the same day as Hughes and had lived at 72 Church Street. He was firstly part of the National Reserve, then in the Defence Corps and joined up in September 1914. He was sent to Stowmarket to guard the explosives factory. He was transferred to the 2nd Suffolks in 1916, and went to France in December of that year. He was wounded in Belgium in September 1917 both in the shoulder and internally. He was in hospital in Netley for two months and was never passed fit again for service. He went to Felixstowe and then to Rugeoy(?) where he died from the effects of his wounds received in Belgium. He left a widow and seven children.

On the Second World War Memorial in Lavenham Church there is only one name bearing the same name as one of those who died in the previous war, which is Dent. He was probably one of the children of George Dent and had been born in 1916. He was killed in a flying accident over the North Sea while serving with the R.A.F. before the Battle of Britain began.

Of the seventy-six men who died in the First World War not surprisingly as many as fifty-six of them died in France (fifty) and Belgium (six). The Gallipoli Peninsula claimed the lives of six men, Gaza in Palestine three, Port Said one and Mesopotamia one. One died in Italy and one at sea. Seven died in hospital in the United Kingdom.

These men lived mainly in the following streets: Prentice Street – twelve, High Street – twelve, Water Street – eleven, Church Street – seven, Bolton Street – five, Hall Road – four, Market Place – five and Shilling Street – two. There were sixteen other men who lived at other addresses in the area in and around Lavenham and one at Skipton, Yorkshire. If one walks around Lavenham today one can soon find most of the houses that the First World War servicemen lived in, only one is not purely residential and that is one in Water Street which is now an Art Gallery. The houses are usually small town or terraced houses or small cottages. They are mostly made of brick and unpretentious. One or two are typical Lavenham timbered houses.

The town was still prosperous from its traditional industries at the outbreak of the war but a few years later a severe slump set in, mainly brought about by the decline and closure of the local weaving industry on which the town had depended for nearly six hundred years. In 1930 the factories were closed down and the looms stood empty. No serious attempt to provide alternative employment was made and the population which had been hard hit by the war casualties declined further to a figure of 1,400 in 1936. Electricity had arrived in 1934 and its ugly poles were removed after a continuous battle with the authorities in the 1970s. It makes a tremendous visual difference to the small town.

The main industry of Lavenham today is the tourist industry and the town is much admired by visitors from all over the world as a marvellous example of what a Suffolk wool town used to look like.

The Electoral Roll of 1987 had the names of 1,447 people on it. It is very interesting to see that many of the family names are still local residents and no doubt related to the dead men of the First World War.

The biggest family is the Faires family with as many as twenty names on the roll, others are Aldous (7), Long (6), Pryke (6), Twitchett (5), Poulson (5), Archer (4), Mills (4), Fayers (4), Eady (3), Sturgeon (3), Rampling (3), Butcher (2), Hunt (2), Steward (2), and several others. To sum up about a quarter of the names on the war memorial in Lavenham Church are the names of families who are still living in Lavenham today.

Bibliography

G. H. Lenox-Conyngham, *Lavenham War Memorial Book*, in Lavenham Church.

Soldiers Died in the Great War, H.M.S.O., no date.

Capt. A. Fair, M.C. and Capt. E. D. Wolton, compilers *The History of the 1/5th Battalion The Suffolk Regiment*, Eyre and Spotiswoode, 1923.

C. C. R. Murphy, *The History of the Suffolk Regiment 1914–1927*, Hutchinson, 1928.

Kelly's Directory of Suffolk of 1912.

Kelly's Directory of Suffolk of 1916.

F. Lingard Ranson 'Lavenham Suffolk', *East Anglian Daily Times*, Ipswich, 1937.

G. H. Lenox-Conyngham, *Lavenham in War Time 1914–18*, no date.

G. H. Lenox-Conyngham, *Lavenham 11th November, 1918 – The Day of the Signing of the Armistice*, 1918.